CHECKS AND BALANCES WON'T SAVE US NOW.

WHAT WILL?

BOSTON REVIEW

Publisher & Coeditor-in-Chief Deborah Chasman

Coeditor-in-Chief Joshua Cohen

Executive Editor Matt Lord

Associate Editor Cameron Avery

Contributing Editors Thomas Ferguson, Adom Getachew, Jake Grumbach, Lily Hu, Robin D. G. Kelley, Becca Rothfeld, & Simon Torracinta

Editorial Assistant Harrison Knight

Columnist David Austin Walsh

Associate Publisher Jasmine Parmley

Circulation Manager Irina Costache

Finance Manager Anthony DeMusis III

Board of Advisors Derek Schrier (Chair), Margo Beth Fleming, Archon Fung, Deborah Fung, Larry Kramer, Richard M. Locke, Jeff Mayersohn, Scott Nielsen, Robert Pollin, Rob Reich, Hiram Samel, Kim Malone Scott, Brandon M. Terry, & Michael Voss

Print Design Rest Design

Cover Design Alex Camlin

Checks and Balances Won't Save Us Now is *Boston Review* issue 2025.2 (Forum 34 / 50.2 under former designation system).

Printed and bound in the United States by Sheridan.

Distributed by Haymarket Books (www.haymarketbooks.org) to the trade in the U.S. through Consortium Book Sales and Distribution (www.cbsd.com) and internationally through Ingram Publisher Services International (www.ingramcontent.com).

To become a member,
visit bostonreview.net/memberships.

For questions about donations and major gifts,contact Irina Costache at irina@bostonreview.net.

For questions about memberships,
email members@bostonreview.net.

Boston Review
PO Box 390568
Cambridge, MA 02139

ISSN: 0734-2306 / ISBN: 978-1-946511-95-9

CONTENTS | SPRING 2025

THIS ISSUE IS the first of *Boston Review*'s fiftieth anniversary year. You'll find a forum on the constitutional crisis at the heart of this dangerous moment for the country and a bold new design. And in a special archival feature—the first of fifty to appear in print and online—John Ganz introduces our Summer 2000 essay "On Post-Fascism," by the late philosopher and one-time member of Hungarian Parliament G. M. Tamás. It has proven "one of the most prescient and insightful political texts of the new century," Ganz writes.

The first issue of *BR* appeared in June 1975. The magazine was then called *New Boston Review*, published by a small nonprofit and focused on literature and the arts. Vol. 1, No. 1 was 32 pages and sold for 75 cents, in tabloid format, with Susan Sontag in the front and classifieds in the back. In 1991, with *New* gone from the name, the magazine took a sharp editorial turn. Politics had always been in our pages—Sontag spoke frankly of Vietnam just months after the war ended—but we resolved that it would now be our beating heart. We were inspired by Noam Chomsky's 1967 essay, "The Responsibility of Intellectuals." Intellectuals are a privileged group, Chomsky argued, and with those privileges come large responsibilities—chief among them, "to speak the truth and expose lies."

We embraced that responsibility and saw it as part of a broader commitment to a radically more democratic and egalitarian society. So we focused increasingly on political argument—examining imperial escapades that have done so much damage, addressing inequalities of class, race, and gender, and proposing paths to a better future. Our format shifted too. Because ideas grow stronger through dialogue, we brought people into conversation about what justice requires and how best to realize it. The result became our signature feature—the forum—which confronts seemingly intractable challenges with new ideas and perspectives.

We are proud of what we've accomplished over fifty years, but we will not be celebrating with a lavish gala. At a time of spiraling authoritarianism, our democratic purpose is more urgent than ever. We face an autocratic executive eroding basic liberties, usurping legislative and judicial power, targeting the most vulnerable in spectacular displays of cruelty—and hoping to crush independent institutions, free expression, and critical thought. We will celebrate by standing up for precisely those things, publishing work that keeps faith with the democratic commitments that serve as our north star.

That begins with this issue's forum. Amid Trump's brazen attacks, courts have played a leading role in resistance. Political scientist Lisa L. Miller warns that liberal hopes in such checks and balances are misplaced. Far from a safeguard of democracy, she argues, America's constitutional order has always been at odds with it. Too many checks and balances are the problem, breeding the dysfunction that got us here. Powerful elites exploit our fragmented system of government to block desperately needed reforms, and only political movements that recognize these obstacles and mobilize large majorities can get us beyond the status quo. Respondents disagree about how to build a successful movement and the best way to make our political institutions more responsive to ordinary people. But all are clear that we face a serious crisis and must respond accordingly.

Elsewhere in the issue, Judith Levine reports on mutual aid as resistance, Troy Nahumko writes from Spain on the far right's war on memory, and Debbie Nathan traces the insidious history of the national security exception fueling Trump's deportation machine. Alex Gourevitch mounts a vigorous defense of the right to protest on campus. And Vietnam veteran David Cortright explains how the peace movement built broad-based support—changing the course of the Vietnam War in ways that they couldn't predict.

Writing a quarter-century ago, Tamás foresaw the "post-totalitarian fascism" that now exists without stormtroopers or a one-party system. "Cutting the civic and human community in two," he writes— "this is fascism." With their calls for solidarity and a truly inclusive democracy, our contributors offer a vision for a way forward. **BR**

Still from security camera footage of Rümeysa Öztürk's abduction by ICE agents. Image: AP

MUTUAL AID IN THE AGE OF FASCISM

Judith Levine

AROUND SUNSET ON MARCH 25, Fatema Ahmad, executive director of the grassroots Muslim Justice League in Boston, was winding down after a call with a group of attorneys. They had been strategizing their response to a widening pattern of "foreign student abductions"—unwarned Immigration and Customs Enforcement (ICE) arrests based on allegations of support of terrorism, a.k.a. protest of Israel's war on Gaza. "We're a city with a lot of universities," said Ahmad. "We knew it was going to happen here."

And then it did. Not two hours after the meeting, Ahmad got an email from one of the lawyers, Mahsa Khanbabai, informing her that she'd just gotten her first student abduction case. Right then the phone rang. It was Danny Timpona, an organizer from Neighbor to Neighbor, a twenty-eight-year-old "base-building" organization that works on immigrant, racial, and environmental justice in cities across Massachusetts. Neighbor to Neighbor is helming a statewide ICE watch hotline called LUCE. On March 25 it was barely two weeks old.

"At about 5:30 a guy called in from Somerville, frantically saying, 'Someone is being kidnapped,'" Timpona told me. The hotline operator asked the routine questions: *What did you see? What is the address where you saw it? Did you witness it yourself or hear about it secondhand?* They determined the report was more than credible—it was urgent. Within five minutes, LUCE's rapid responders were on the scene.

Timpona and Ahmad quickly established that the first abduction case and the kidnap victim were the same person: Rümeysa Öztürk, a Turkish Tufts University PhD student on a valid visa who'd been surrounded by masked plainclothes officers, handcuffed, and hustled into an unmarked car. The officers did not show their IDs—which revealed them to be ICE agents—until after they'd taken her phone and backpack and restrained her. And, although a federal judge ordered that night that Öztürk could not be removed from the state or the country until a court ruled on jurisdictional matters, ICE had already driven her to a detention facility in northeastern Vermont and the next day to a notoriously brutal private ICE detention lockup in Louisiana; her visa had been revoked without notice four days before the arrest. Öztürk's offense: coauthoring an op-ed in the student newspaper urging the university to divest from Israel.

LUCE's rapid responders have three tasks: verify, document, witness. They were not rapid enough to do the last one; Öztürk's abduction had taken less than two minutes. But they could verify and document. Canvassing door to door, they learned that two unmarked vehicles had been parked in the area for two days. Neighbors showed them phone videos, but most were illegible. Then someone contributed their building's front-door surveillance video. In it, Öztürk's face is recognizable, the agents' efficient movements chillingly clear. "The fact that you can hear Rümeysa screaming makes it particularly horrifying," noted Ahmad.

Öztürk was not rescued. Intervention is never the aim any-way, Neighbor to Neighbor's executive director, Dálida Rocha, told me; especially under a Trump regime operating with new aggression and impunity, that's too risky. In fact, verification and documentation are the most important parts of the process. They do nothing less than free the community for something like normal life. The chaos and ran-domness of ICE's arrests under Trump II are causing terror in immigrant neighborhoods. Panic fuels rumors and misinformation, which in turn exacerbate panic. People worry: *Should I take the kids to school, show up at work, shop at the bodega?* The insecurity may become so overwhelm-ing that they "self-deport" —which, of course, is the point of ICE's terror campaign.

In one instance, someone thought they saw ICE agents lurking outside an elementary school; they made a TikTok, which went viral. Parents were scared. Through loose community networks, LUCE got wind of the rumor and sent verifiers, who chatted with teachers, parents, and neighbors and determined that ICE was not and had not been in the school's vicinity. They relayed the intelligence back to LUCE and other trusted community leaders, who corrected the misinformation by word of mouth and social media. The TikTok was taken down —and relative calm was renewed. Reliable information allows people to assess risks rationally. In the context of collective action, all this builds "power over fear," Rocha told me.

The video of the abduction obtained by LUCE proved invaluable far beyond Somerville. Released to the press, it became a major story, published, posted, and reposted around the world. Some who lived under authoritarian regimes saw a familiar tactic: a disappearance. No matter how long it takes to yield justice, witness must be borne, said Timpona: "Visibility is accountability."

THE COORDINATED RESPONSE to Öztürk's kidnapping exemplifies community self-defense and mutual aid at their best. Timpona and Ahmad were connected by a comrade in LUCE's network of grassroots or-ganizations. The frightened caller contacted a friend, who recommended the hotline, which he'd heard about by word of mouth. That the first impulse was to call a community organization, not the police, was itself a kind of win.

The Boston housing rights nonprofit City Life/Vida Urbana defines mutual aid as "networks of people in a community voluntarily supporting one another with resources and services, such as providing food and housing, financial support, education around and connection to government and social service systems, and more. It is based on the principles of solidarity and collectivism rather than profit and individualism."

When anyone can be summoned by the state to extract information, "people lose their social instincts."

Mutual aid is the brigade of volunteers mucking out basements after a flood, the church basement food pantry staffed by retirees, the GoFundMe to pay the rent for a tenant about to be evicted. It can look like an easier alternative to politics, which requires not just generosity but toughness, not just tolerance but side-taking.

But mutual aid is more than glorified good neighborliness. The response to the Somerville abduction is a case in point: such projects can channel rage and fear into disciplined, concrete action, linking movements and bringing new individuals into them. Rather than sidestep politics, it can make politics happen. The LUCE group encompasses immigrant rights and tenants' rights, prison abolition and workplace safety; it unites communities from Asians and Pacific Islanders to Dominicans, Muslims to Unitarians.

And it links activists across distances. LUCE was born under the guidance of Siembra NC, an immigrant rights and anti-wage theft nonprofit, which also helped groups in Missouri, South Carolina, Kentucky, Kansas, and Texas establish hotlines and learn to run engaging and effective know-your-rights "parties." And Siembra, in turn, has learned from other groups. At the top of its YouTube page is "LA Fights Back," a witty riff on why ICE can't find enough people to deport that lifts up the Los Angeles Community Self-Defense Coalition. The coalition conducts daily patrols seeking ICE vehicles, sends out social media alerts, and waits for defenders to arrive. One person with a bullhorn telling residents to bolt the doors can sometimes be enough to torpedo a raid. *Siembra* means *seeding*.

Bridging racial and generational divides, coordinating ad hoc good works into workable systems, cultivating leadership, mutual aid builds progressive movements for the long haul. As we learned from the COVID pandemic, the dynamics forged by crisis can last after the crisis has passed. A 2024 report authored by several community groups in East Boston found that the collective response to the needs of the community—distributing 5,000 cooked meals per week; donating everything from diapers to furniture; driving people to the hospital; convening healing circles and gratitude ceremonies—strengthened existing collaborations, sparked new ones, and "dissolved some silos." Informants "emphasized the importance of relationships and trust as the building blocks of this work," in which "practices of reciprocity and mutuality . . . shifted mindsets away from one-way dependence on charity towards recognizing that everyone has the capacity to give and to receive."

FOR ACTIVISTS LOOKING to history for inspiration, Communists and fellow travelers during the Great Depression offer plenty. Much of their local organizing centered around the twin scourges of unemployment and eviction. When landlords hired marshals to throw unemployed tenants and their belongings onto the street, nonviolent eviction resistance squads put their bodies in the way and the families back into their homes.

In *Invisible Man*, Ralph Ellison's unnamed protagonist comes upon two white men carrying the shabby belongings of an elderly Black woman onto the street as she weeps, pleads, and pummels the chest of one of them. The narrator is shocked, infuriated by the racism of the scene, then ashamed to be watching without intervening. As he is drawn into a spontaneous act of collective resistance, shock turns to exhilaration, racialized rage to cross-racial solidarity, and mutual aid to politics. "Men, women and children seized articles and dashed inside shouting, laughing," he reports. "It was like a holiday. I didn't want it to stop." As the action intensifies, a white man shouts: "Why don't we march?" The narrator, and the rest of the crowd, seconds: "Let's march!"

The actions were not always nonviolent. During the Great Rent Strike War of 1932 in the Bronx, landlords brought in police and marshals to force tenants from the buildings. Hundreds of protesters there to defend the strike fought the police hand to hand.

Such interventions were both numerous and effective. Between November 1931 and June 1932 New York saw some 186,000 evictions. But many tenants were rehoused by popular force. According to Richard Boyer and Herbert Morais in *Labor's Untold Story,* the Communist Party's Unemployed Council moved 77,000 families back into their homes, at least until the next dispossession.

Similar actions were taking place around the world. In Sydney, for instance, the Communist-led Unemployed Workers' Movement (UWM), which numbered in the thousands, turned rehousing efforts into weeks-long occupations. Always more than an army of furniture movers, the UWM suffused its mutual aid with political analysis, in leaflets and street corner orations "blam[ing] the profit-driven chaos of capitalism for the destitution facing millions," wrote Eddie Stephenson on *Red Flag*, an Australian socialist newspaper.

For neighborhood groups in the United States, mutual aid was not an end in itself either. The persistent rent strikes and eviction resistance, coupled with political agitation, pushed Congress to enact the Housing Act of 1937—the precursor to the Department of Housing and Urban Development—which provided loans to local agencies to build low-rent public housing. Activism also led to the passage of the Emergency Price Control Act of 1942, which established caps on allowable rents nationwide. While that law expired in 1947, some states and cities kept rent controls in place. Meanwhile, the federal government kept building public housing for low-income tenants—which was racially segregated until the Fair Housing Act of 1968. (In 1974 President Nixon placed a moratorium on public housing construction, and the feds got out of the building business for good.)

Mutual aid and legislative or electoral campaigns require different systems and skills—and both take resources. It's not always easy to do them simultaneously. In 2024 Siembra paid a small army of canvassers, who, along with volunteers, knocked 125,000 voters' doors for Kamala

Harris. We know how that turned out. For Andrew Willis Garcés, who co-founded Siembra eight years ago, the Democrats' fiasco brought up perennial questions about that tension. At the time it seemed obvious that Siembra had to put all hands, and a lot of dollars, on deck to defeat Trump. Yet "without more for thousands of paid canvassers to talk about beyond repeating the uninspiring message from the top of the ballot, Harris still lost," he wrote in a self-critical post-election piece in *In These Times*.

Some organizations managed to balance the two. "In Los Angeles, where tenant organizers have aggressively worked to build public support for local and statewide policies to bring down the cost of rent," wrote Garcés, "those organizers used their door-knocking muscle to win funds for homelessness prevention and help a tenants rights attorney unseat a sitting council member whom they saw as pro-landlord." Siembra also had some electoral victories of their own. In nine of North Carolina's ten most populous counties, voters replaced Republican sheriffs who were enthusiastically arresting immigrants and locking them in local jails with "people who are much more protective of public safety"—and the Constitution, Co-Director Nikki Marín Baena told me.

A FASCIST SOCIETY is one in which some people are deputized to do violence, and everyone else is forced to defend themselves. Those who have lived under an authoritarian regime know how it weakens collective self-defense. "Nothing binds people together more than complicity in the same crime," wrote Nadezhda Mandelstam of life in Stalinist Russia. "The more people could be implicated and compromised, the more traitors, informers, and police spies there were, the greater would be the number of people supporting the regime and longing for it to last thousands of years." When anyone can be summoned by the state to extract information, she continued, "people lose their social instincts, the ties between them weaken, everybody retires to his corner and keeps his mouth shut—which is a great boon to the authorities."

In extorting media outlets that have reported on Trump's crimes and law firms that have helped to prosecute him, the administration achieves one of the goals Mandelstam describes: turning perceived enemies into cowed collaborators. In demanding that universities name names of the foreign students who've engaged in protest and withdrawing cultural grants whose applicants used verboten words like "woman" and "inequity," it shuts mouths. In eliminating every government agency and program that encourages cooperation or empathy, it advances the third, most pernicious, aim: to break social ties.

If we are to have any hope of surviving the coming dark age, we need mutual aid—not just to keep people housed and fed, but to keep them connected.

It makes sense that immigrant communities, who are in the most drastic danger, have been the first to organize. They were ready anyway, having worked to keep each other safe for years of draconian immigration policy—during Obama's, Biden's, and Trump's terms—before today's cruel, spectacular assaults. Other existing mutual aid networks are girding against the Republicans' next salvos. The feminist underground that has been distributing abortion pills into red states since the bans began is figuring out how to continue its work while protecting its members and the pregnant people they serve in the face of heightened surveillance and penalties. The activists know one thing: even if the Comstock Act is resurrected, they will not stop.

Still more mutual aid formations and institutions will need to be born, or reborn. The Department of Agriculture has canceled over $1 billion in funding for two programs that link local farms with food pantries and public school cafeterias. We need farmers' cooperatives based in agrarian socialism. Daycare and afterschool programs are under the knife; Christian nationalism is creeping into curricula. Bring back the free school movement of the 1960s. Health and Human Services is closing the Administration for Community Living, which has helped frail elders and people with disabilities live at home, not in institutions. Because caregiving will be even more privatized than it is now (and we won't have immigrants to do it cheap), the burdens will revert to the family, particularly women. What will family mutual aid look like? Communal, intergenerational housing, shared kitchens, child care shifts, leaving free time for creativity and leisure: let new forms of intimacy and interdependence supplant the patriarchal nuclear family religious fundamentalists and their elected officials have been laboring to reinvigorate for decades.

Mutual aid is not "a thousand points of light," George H. W. Bush's euphemism for replacing the public social safety net with charity. There is no substitute for the state, whose obligation is to redistribute the nation's wealth for the greater good of the greatest number of people. But when the state is a malevolent kleptocracy, mutual aid—neighbors helping neighbors—starts to look like radical civil disobedience, less a thousand points of light than a brilliant beam shining toward a different world. **BR**

KILL IT WITH FIRE

The global right's war on memory

Troy Nahumko

I N AUGUST 1936, after a failed coup against the Second Spanish Republic, Francisco Franco's Nationalist forces seized the city of Badajoz in the western region of Extremadura. The siege was swift, brutal, and indiscriminate. Thousands were executed, soldiers and civilians alike, their bodies stacked and set ablaze. Unbothered by cartographer's lines, the smoke rose in thick, dark columns and drifted across the Caya river, clinging to clothes, hair, and memory.

From Elvas, just across the border, Portuguese civilians and foreign journalists watched the flames and breathed in the evidence of atrocity. The city that once hosted imperialism's genteel mapmakers now served as a front-row seat to mechanized butchery. It was here, in these borderlands, that *Chicago Tribune* correspondent Jay Allen found himself documenting what would become one of the most horrific episodes of the Spanish Civil War.

"This is the most painful story it has ever been my lot to handle," he dispatched in late August. Just days before, Allen had managed to secure an interview with the rebel general himself in Tétouan, Morocco. When asked, "How long, now that your coup has failed in its objectives, is the massacre to go on?" the dictator-in-waiting answered, "There can be no compromise, no truce. . . . I shall save Spain from Marxism at whatever cost."

Allen sought clarification. "That means that you will have to shoot half Spain?" To which Franco replied, "I repeat, at whatever cost."

More than a massacre, Badajoz was a preview. Advancing north, the Nationalist forces became what one historian calls a "column of death," carving a path of blood and fire as they traveled up the Vía de la Plata toward Madrid. During three years of civil war, the province became both graveyard and laboratory—a proving ground for industrialized brutality, which Franco's Nazi allies would later export across Europe.

Victory for the Nationalists came in 1939 and would last for thirty-six years. But the ghosts of Francoism—and of its victims—outlived the regime's apparent passing. Today a low-level war still rages on this terrain, but with a much less visible target: the consciousness and soul of Spain itself. The fire this time burns through memory, as a new generation of Spain's leaders seeks to master what the people are allowed to remember—mirroring far-right movements across Europe and beyond.

UNLIKE COUNTLESS ATROCITIES buried by silence, Badajoz had witnesses. The brutality in Extremadura almost certainly would have vanished into historical footnotes were it not for the foreign correspondents who crossed the border to report beyond the reach of censors.

Alongside colleagues from French and British publications, Allen and the *New York Herald Tribune*'s John T. Whitaker documented the horrors in real time. Their dispatches, splashed across front pages from Lisbon to Paris and London to New York, converted rumor into documented fact. António Salazar's fledgling regime in Portugal also sent correspondents—with clear instructions to favor the rebel cause—but no spin could soften the horror. Even the sanctioned pens of a compliant press could not suppress the sensory weight of what journalists saw.

Franco and his commanders learned quickly from the PR disaster. While abstract slogans about purging Reds and disciplining strikers still resounded in the corridors of power, the photographs and reports transformed local atrocity into global indignation, briefly tilting global opinion toward Madrid's democratically elected government. But only for a moment. Over the ensuing three years of war, the world's great democracies—Britain, France, the United States—chose a posture of strategic indifference, eyes wide shut as Nazi Germany and Fascist Italy helped the Nationalists modernize terror against civilian populations. Their only real concern? That no one challenge Capital. "We English hate fascism," British prime minister Stanley Baldwin reportedly told a colleague in 1936, "but we loathe Bolshevism as much."

Meanwhile, to ensure there would be no more journalists bearing witness from across the Caya, Franco unleashed a brutal campaign of censorship and propaganda that blanketed Spain in silence for decades. The border became not just a line between nations but a fault line between truth and control, the reek of reality and the mask of ideology.

Spain's so-called transition to democracy was framed as a triumph of moderation. It was more like negotiated amnesia.

Of course, the world would soon have other evidence of where fascist ideologies lead: genocide, world war, the mechanized annihilation of entire peoples. But this terror was both exposed and over by 1945. Franco died thirty years later, and he did so peacefully in his bed clutching the mummified hand of Saint Teresa—not at the end of a rope or before a tribunal, but swaddled in power to the very last breath. Fascism in Spain was not defeated. It simply ran out of time.

In its aftermath, the so-called transition to democracy was framed as a triumph of moderation, a masterclass in political compromise. In reality, it was more like negotiated amnesia. King Juan Carlos, hand-picked by Franco himself, inherited not just the throne but the delicate machinery of authoritarian rule. He opened the country to the world, yes—but held tight to his lifetime mandate. To move forward, Spain decided not to look back. Instead of reckoning with the dictatorship's crimes, the government signed a contract with silence. The *Pacto del Olvido*—the Pact of Forgetting—was agreed upon by both the left and the right. No trials. No truth commissions. No accountability. It was a political ceasefire disguised as healing.

Entire generations of Spaniards thus grew up with no real understanding of what happened between 1936 and 1975. Schools more or less skirted the subject. Textbooks tiptoed around atrocity or simply omitted it. In many homes, the only history available came from aging fascist grandparents who romanticized the regime and recited myths polished by decades of propaganda. The Pact didn't just suppress the past; it created a breeding ground where lies could flourish.

But forgetting is not the same as forgiving, and silence is not peace. The truth was not gone—it was being forced to whisper.

ONE MORNING IN 1978, someone left a bit of folk poetry on the wall outside the house of Felisa Casatejada. She ran the butcher's shop in a small village tucked into the scorched plains of Badajoz. The message, daubed in paint with the subtlety of a brick, read: "En casa de la carnicera se venden huesos rojos para el cocido." *At the butcher's house, red bones are sold for stew.*

The villagers had done the unthinkable. For the first time since the civil war, a mass grave of Republican soldiers was exhumed. Bones had surfaced; history had spoken. Like all good truths, this one started in the dirt and spread. But with political leaders so reluctant to confront the past, the movement it spawned would take time.

The *Ley de Memoria Histórica*, passed in 2007, marked a turning point. It acknowledged the victims of Franco's regime, allocated funding for exhumations, and ordered the removal of fascist symbols from public spaces. The children and grandchildren of the silenced started to dig—sometimes with spades, sometimes with subpoenas. Across Spain, quiet hills and fallow fields began to give up their secrets: mass graves hidden under olive groves, along roadside ditches, behind crumbling walls. Bodies stacked like firewood, wrapped in remnants of uniforms or Sunday clothes. Toothbrushes and wedding rings. Rosaries. According to official figures from the Ministry of Justice, there are 2,567 mass graves throughout the country and more than 114,000 missing persons waiting to be identified.

With these exhumations comes the smell. Not literal anymore, not always. But something unmistakable—the whiff of old violence, of unfinished business. The air carries a moral weight, an atmosphere thick with the recognition of justice long denied. It began to cling again—to national identity, to civic memory. In newspaper headlines about unearthed graves. In classrooms where students ask why they never learned about the war and turn to twisted Youtubers to fill the void left by silence. In bitter debates over statues, street names, and the mausoleum at the Valley of the Fallen, which Franco had built as a memorial to all who died in the civil war and where the dictator himself was interred.

Even cinema caught the scent. Pedro Almodóvar's 2021 film *Parallel Mothers* ends not with a kiss or twist but with the slow, methodical exhumation of a Civil War mass grave. No dialogue, no fanfare: just dirt, bones, and the dignity of those who had waited eighty years to be counted. In a country still allergic to the word "dictatorship," it was a more radical act than any speech. The scene does what the state long wouldn't: it looks. It listens. It kneels.

Almodóvar didn't just tell a story—he staged a reckoning. The following year, the *Ley de Memoria Democrática* was passed, taking a more assertive approach to dealing with the legacy of the Franco regime. While the earlier law left much of the heavy lifting to families and volunteer associations, the new law finally put the state in charge of locating the disappeared—something it had been politely avoiding for decades. The legislation went further by declaring the Franco regime illegal, annulling its political convictions, and introducing penalties for glorifying the dictatorship. The message was clear: Spain had decided, democratically, that the best way to move on is to actually confront its past. And since then the soil has continued to shift. The provincial government of Cáceres, together with the Asociación Memorial en el Cementerio de Cáceres, recently announced a bold plan: to exhume the estimated three hundred victims from a mass grave in the town's cemetery by 2026—just shy of a century after their deaths.

All this was a start, but it was also deeply contested. Today, half a century after the return of democracy, efforts to name the nameless and rebury the forgotten meet growing resistance. Opening graves opens wounds, it is said. The grandchildren of the vanquished search for the dead while the genealogical and ideological heirs of the executioners memorialize the old regime and seek to rehabilitate Franco's legacy. Instead of uniforms, they are dressed in suits and seated in parliaments. Their ideas are vintage—hierarchy, purity, obedience—but their delivery has gotten an upgrade: polished videos, algorithmic outrage, history by rigged newsfeed. What was once declared by firing squad is now spoken into microphones and retweeted into relevance.

That's just what happened last month when MP Sergio Rodríguez, speaking in the Balearic Parliament as a member of the far-right, ultra-nationalist Vox party, invoked April 1, 1939—the day Franco declared the Civil War over—not as a solemn end to a national tragedy, but as a triumph. He stood at the people's podium and called it Victory Day.

BORN IN THE AFTERMATH of the 2008 financial crisis and midwifed by generational denial, Vox has seized on this buried legacy, positioning itself as guardian of the country's "true history." Through leverage in parliamentary coalitions, its members have dragged the traditional right—the Partido Popular (PP), founded by ex-Francoist ministers but traditionally wary of outright revisionism—ever closer to its roots. In regions where Vox has gained power, it has made it its mission to roll back memory laws, strip away funding for disinterments, and reconsecrate silence.

When exhumations at the Valley of the Fallen were announced in 2019, Vox sued to stop them, decrying political "vengeance." The sentiment is that "the civilized thing to do is not to disturb the repose of the dead," as one party member later put it. When allies in Andalusia erased memorials to Franco's victims, another Vox leader explained, "We won't pay to spread lies." Plaques honoring Republicans executed by Franco's forces were removed in Madrid after a conservative-led city council halted a memorial project, arguing that victims from both sides of the Civil War should be honored and QR codes should be used in place of names.

In these erasures, Old Testament rhetoric has become a weapon of choice. Vox president Santiago Abascal frames the nation as a divinely ordained Promised Land needing salvation from "invaders" (immigrants, secularists, feminists). At rallies he speaks of the sacred fatherland while evoking Santiago Matamoros—St. James the Moor-slayer—and a new Reconquista, the Christian holy war that expelled Muslims and culminated in Catholic monarchy.

And so the cycle threatens to begin again—not with tanks in the streets, but with language in the legislature. Not with mass graves freshly dug, but with old ones left sealed in the name of "reconciliation" and letting sleeping dogs lie, as long as they are on one side.

Far-right manifestos to this effect proliferate. The latest, published in March, begins "We, Spaniards grateful to Franco, want to raise our voice." It was signed by more than 1,200 people, among them 1981 coup leader Antonio Tejero, *Manos Limpias* (*Clean Hands*) chief Miguel Bernad Remón, retired judges, and military officers. Praising the "prosperity" of the dictatorship while blithely ignoring its repression, it is part of a larger effort—Platform 2025—to protest the government's plans to commemorate the transition to democracy on the semicentennial of Franco's death later this year.

In Extremadura in particular, the regional president, PP member María Guardiola, initially made strong statements against the extreme right. In June 2023, after regional elections, she declared, "I cannot let into government those who deny sexist violence, those who are dehumanizing immigrants, and those who throw the LGTBI flag in the trash." Pressed by a journalist, she insisted: "I am a woman of my word. . . . I will not govern with Vox." But her word didn't last a news cycle. By July, under Madrid's orders, she had promptly signed a coalition agreement. The chance to steal away a traditionally socialist fiefdom was too important to squander.

Now, the regional government has sought to repeal the *Ley de Memoria Democrática*. In its place, leaders have drafted a "Concordia Law" that erases distinctions between victims and perpetrators, halts exhumations, purges uncomfortable words, and promotes a sanitized narrative of Spain's past. "Dictatorship" has been disappeared and would no longer appear in official language. "Repression" has vanished. Even the word "Francoism" is gone. The effect is not just revisionism but ritual erasure: a kind of political dry cleaning, laundering history until it smells like nothing at all.

The move reflects a national pattern. From Castilla y León to Valencia, Vox has successfully pressured the PP to dismantle historical memory policies. With these new lords, the word "memory" itself becomes suspect. In textbooks, in museums, on public plaques, reality is bleached, the past reduced to neutral nouns and fuzzy abstractions. A massacre becomes a "conflict." A coup against a democratically elected government and an ensuing war against it becomes a "difference of opinion."

THESE PATTERNS of institutional forgetting—the control of language, the reframing of history, the bureaucratic scrubbing of uncomfortable truths—travel with alarming ease. In the United States, built on its own mass graves and selective amnesia, the same techniques are being deployed under Trump—and likewise in concert with people who once condemned him. "Trump makes people I care about afraid. Immigrants, Muslims, etc." J. D. Vance wrote in 2016. "Because of this I find him reprehensible. God wants better of us." On Facebook, he worried to a friend that Trump might be "America's Hitler."

Now, with Vance's blessing, the Trump administration has deemed hundreds of words and phrases off-limits, from "accessible" and "diversity" to "LGBT" and "vulnerable populations." The full list amounts to a thesaurus of evasion, each edit a tiny shovel of dirt over the graves of truth. In a stealth act of jingoism, the Department of Defense recently sanitized a page dedicated to Ira Hayes, a Native American Marine immortalized in one of the most iconic images in American history: the flag raising at Iwo Jima. "Discriminatory Equity Ideology is a form of Woke cultural Marxism that has no place in our military," the Pentagon's press secretary explained.

Meanwhile, the Department of Education is to be closed entirely. The head of the National Archives was fired, replaced for now by Secretary of State Marco Rubio. The Pentagon is halting extremism training aimed at rooting out white nationalism in the military. The U.S. Naval Academy removed Maya Angelou's *I Know Why the Caged Bird Sings* from its library—while *Mein Kampf*, of course, remains. Even the Department of Agriculture now polices its lexicon, stripping "equity" from grant programs. All in the name of "restoring truth and sanity to American history," as one executive order puts it, railing against "divisive narratives."

And that's just at the federal level. In red states, the erasure has been less red tape and more chainsaw. In Florida, students are told that slavery "developed skills" among the enslaved. The state's Stop WOKE Act bans lessons that might cause "psychological distress," particularly for those most comforted by history in its heavily edited form. A Texas school district insists we teach "both sides" of the Holocaust, while Oklahoma mandates the Ten Commandments.

In all this, the past isn't just contested. It's being actively dismantled, manipulated, weaponized—hollowed out and repackaged as a white nationalist fable in which oppression is at best a footnote, and fascism just another policy preference.

THE *PACTO DEL OLVIDO* had its American counterpart in the Lost Cause myth—the decades of Confederate memorials framing traitors as heroes and slavery as a "states' rights" dispute. Now, the GOP accelerates the lie. The same party that bans books now lauds Viktor Orbán's "illiberal democracy," a phrase also used to describe Franco's black-and-white Spain. In April, Mississippi Governor Tate Reeves declared Confederate Heritage Month—indulging, for the thirty-second time, an annual request from the Sons of Confederate Veterans to memorialize their legacy.

Never reckoning with its own past, America, it seems, is now sharing Spain's fate. No truth commissions, no reparations. Instead, fierce backlash to memory—"It appears the purpose of the 1619 Project is to delegitimize America," a *Federalist* writer contended—and narratives of a nation invaded.

To say nothing of the flames. Last year, a fervent Trump supporter running for office in Missouri filmed herself setting two books ablaze. Three months later, Christian nationalist podcaster Stew Peters implored his hundreds of thousands of followers "to go into these public schools and rip the filth off of these shelves and destroy it. To remove it from the face of the planet for all of eternity, to turn it to ash." Asked by *Newsweek* for a statement, he replied: "Kill it with fire."

But the air remembers what the textbooks omit and the strongmen burn. The unmarked graves in Tulsa, chain gangs in Alabama, caged children at the border—their history will outlast the censors, as have the truth about Francoism and the course of fascism. The smoke is a sign, and if history doesn't repeat, it does, at the very least, leave a smell. Faint at first. Then lingering. Then impossible to ignore. **BR**

THE DEAD END OF CHECKS AND BALANCES

Lisa L. Miller

With responses from Eric Blanc, Marcus Gadson, Gianpaolo Baiocchi, Samuel Moyn, Aziz Huq, Kelly Hayes & Maya Schenwar, and Lily Geismer. Miller replies.

On the floor of the Senate at the end of January, Chuck Schumer condemned the actions of Donald Trump's new administration. "This is an explicit assault on our system of checks and balances which have served this republic so well for centuries," he stated.

In doing so, Schumer tapped into a hallowed American ideal. Probably no narrative about our system of government is more widely shared than this one: that the Framers of the Constitution wisely restrained government power through separation of powers, judicial review, bicameralism, and federalism. Especially in moments of heightened political conflict, many Americans invoke checks and balances as a safeguard against tyranny and essential protection for minorities. Hillary Clinton captured the essence of the prevailing view when she asserted, after Trump's first win in 2016, that "constitutional checks and balances" are a key part of "an immune system protecting us from the disease of authoritarianism."

It is thus unsurprising to hear Democrats marshalling these ideas against Trump's brazen and ongoing attacks on government, immigrants, and political opponents. What these invocations mean as a practical matter is not always clear, however. Some place their hopes in the courts, even as the administration openly flouts many rulings. Others, taken with the promise of "progressive federalism," urge resistance in blue states. Still others seem eager for a return to "normal," evoking a golden age of bipartisanship and well-functioning constitutionalism before Trump. These strategies have intuitive appeal because they draw on popular ideas about the virtues of our constitutional system, but they miss something fundamental about our political crisis—and thus about how to resolve it.

The fact is, both Schumer's and Clinton's appeals are deeply flawed. Far from serving our republic well, America's unusual system of checks and balances has paralyzed it—contributing to the very authoritarianism we now face rather than protecting us from it. However well-meaning these venerable invocations, doubling down on America's alleged constitutional virtues at this moment will only entrench the dysfunction that got us here. If our aim is to safeguard democracy, these dangerous times call for a long-overdue reckoning with the system's deep vices—and a clear vision for overcoming them.

Indeed, urging a return to normal misses the point that the normal order is widely perceived as a problem. Majorities of Americans across the political spectrum have long understood that their system of government doesn't serve them well. Institutional obstacles at all levels empower elite minorities to safeguard their own interests and block popular policies that would broadly serve the American people, from universal health care to a higher minimum wage. Of course, Trump's attacks on political institutions have little to do with constraining the power of elites or advancing such policies; on the contrary, with Elon Musk at the head of DOGE, they are advancing rank corruption and kleptocracy for the benefit of the ultrawealthy and extreme ideologues. But Trump does tap into the sentiment that our institutions are broken. Acknowledging the flaws in our system does not mean endorsing his, or any president's, unlimited power. Nor does it mean there is no form of checks and balances that can serve American democracy. Rather, it clarifies the necessity and urgency of reforming government so it responds better to the needs of ordinary people.

To advance this goal, we need a frank assessment of how our system of so-called checks and balances works as a real-world set of democratic institutions. The conventional wisdom says that checks and balances forestall the abuse of power. But our particular system constrains the public far more than it constrains elites. By obstructing ambitious political changes, it enables those who benefit from the status quo to protect their powers and privileges. Instead of celebrating this structure, we should recognize that ordinary Americans have been trying to overcome it for two centuries. That, in turn, requires expanding our understanding of checks on power.

It also requires a proactive political agenda. Fortunately, we do not need to reinvent the wheel on this front. U.S. history is full of successful struggles to reduce opportunities for elites to block needed reforms. Labor activists, abolitionists, the civil rights and New Deal coalitions: all have pushed hard against a political structure that protects the "special privileges" of the few, engaging a diverse array of Americans through social movements to make our constitutional system more genuinely democratic. At this dangerous moment for American democracy, their example—not the hallowed appeal to checks and balances—points the way forward.

———————————

THE CORE VALUE of American-style checks and balances is restraint: ensuring that government does not get too powerful and is not monopolized by one set of interests. But the focus on restraint has three major flaws.

First, the checks and balances narrative ignores the dangers of government *inaction*. Democratic governments are supposed to protect basic rights, counteract private power, and advance the public good. But constraining government power does not eliminate the problem of concentrated power. On the contrary, it provides narrowly focused, resource-rich private interests with opportunities to constrain policy reforms that do not serve their interests. Political systems with many checkpoints have a powerful bias in favor of the status quo, which generally benefits elites—particularly economic elites. Such groups and individuals are far more likely to have access to politicians and other powerbrokers than are ordinary people. Every checkpoint is, in effect, a veto, offering political opportunities to stop policy reforms that threaten entrenched interests. Unlike most democracies, the United States has a tremendously high number of constitutional veto points—in the House, Senate, presidency, courts, and state governments.

The upshot is terribly limiting. Successful policy change requires approval from at least a majority (sometimes a supermajority) of law-makers in three separately elected arms of government—the House, the Senate, and the executive. Blocking change requires just enough power in one. Even under the best of circumstances, failure is the most likely outcome. Add in aggressive lobbying by wealthy interests, and obstruc-tion is nearly guaranteed. Since the end of World War II, fewer than 5 percent of bills introduced in Congress have become law. In the Senate, the filibuster means that representatives of a fraction of the public can block popular legislation. And in both houses, large, complex committee structures and obstacles to floor votes further amplify veto points. It's no wonder that studies of lobbying find that it is most effective when it aims to *block* change.

Far from serving our republic well, America's unusual system of checks and balances has paralyzed it.

A standard response to this critique is that checks and balances are designed to force consensus building—a particularly important democratic virtue in a large and diverse country. But if a powerful set of interests benefits from the status quo, why pursue consensus building if simply blocking is an option? That is why so many policies supported by large majorities of Americans (often in both parties) have been blocked at the national level: minimum wage increases; universal, affordable health care; mandated paid family and medical leave; labor protections; immi-gration reform that secures borders but offers opportunities for seasonal workers and pathways to citizenship; universal background checks for firearms purchases.

Even when major policies do get past political checkpoints, they face the veto of the federal courts. In the latter half of the twentieth century, federal courts validated national legislation guaranteeing equal rights for racial minorities and women—laws aimed at state governments that preserved old hierarchies. These successes contributed to a liberal elite consensus that courts, rights, constitutions, and limited government would serve as guardians of progressive politics. But this period was anomalous, and the focus on courts helped to atrophy mass politics. Historically, federal courts have often served elite interests, and in recent decades, as more reactionaries have been appointed to the federal bench, the Supreme Court has weakened congressional legislation on health care, voting rights, labor, campaign finance, environmental protections, and gun safety, among many other policy areas.

The fact that many Americans have more trust in the Supreme Court than any other branch, even with steep declines in that trust over the past decade, highlights the stranglehold the checks and balances narrative still has on the American political imagination. The repeated failure of government to respond to public demands leaves the electorate confused about political accountability and cynical about the political system. The standard checks and balances narrative then leads to doubling down on the very institutions that thwart democratic accountability in the first place.

A second flaw of the checks and balances vision is its unqualified emphasis on protecting political minorities. The glaring oversight is, *which* minorities? The one percent are a political minority, as are corporate leaders, large business owners, and philanthropic and well-funded interest groups, which often represent the preferences of groups and individuals on the upper end of the socioeconomic ladder. Elites, by definition, are a political minority. It is typically these minorities that benefit from checks and balances, and ordinary Americans pay the price.

A good example is the repeated failure to implement universal, affordable health care in the United States. It's not for lack of public support. Some form of universal health insurance has been popular for more than a century. And bills expanding health coverage have been introduced in Congress under nearly every presidential administration since Harry S. Truman's. The "central issue" of his 1948 campaign, Truman said, was "the welfare of all the people *against special privilege for the few.*" Yet today, among high-income countries, the United States is alone in lacking universal health care. It also has the highest infant and maternal mortality rates, the lowest life expectancy at birth, and the highest death rate from causes amenable to health care prevention, even as it spends considerably more.

The most common explanations point to the raw power of the health care lobby, including the American Medical Association (AMA), insurance and pharmaceutical companies, and for-profit hospitals. Others argue that, though public opinion polls can tell us what the public wants in the abstract, they don't account for public opposition to specific policy proposals. Perhaps Americans aren't so keen on universal health insurance after all.

The problem with these explanations is that formidable medical interests, business opposition, and skeptical publics exist in other wealthy democracies, yet the United States is the only one that lacks national, universal health coverage. What distinguishes this country is the unusually complex array of veto opportunities that opponents of health care policy reforms can access. It isn't lack of broad public support that hinders compulsory health insurance; it is the ability of powerful, discreet interests to capitalize on the multitude of checkpoints.

For most of the twentieth century, the AMA, American Hospital Association, and similar groups worked hard to find enough sympathetic lawmakers in one chamber or the other to kill off proposed bills, often by targeting key committee members. Meanwhile, white Democratic lawmakers in the South, eager to keep federal rules and scrutiny away from their deeply segregated and unequal economic institutions (including medical facilities and professions), opposed members of their own party on health care reform. From the early twentieth century through the 1970s, when Democrats controlled either chamber of Congress, Southern Democrats maneuvered themselves into chairing two of the most important committees, the House Ways and Means Committee and the Senate Finance Committee. The convergence of interests between white Southern Democrats and geographically dispersed business elites—groups that hardly represented a majority of Americans, it is worth noting—kept many bills from even making it to a floor vote.

But bills were stymied in other ways as well. In the 1970s, for example, Nixon governed with a Democratic Congress, and a bipartisan health care plan even made it out of the Ways and Means Committee. But Democratic Committee chair Wilbur Mills refused to bring it to a floor vote out of concern that it would not pass the full House, depriving Americans of an opportunity to identify the bill's opponents. In another alliance of strange bedfellows, some powerful Democrats and a few labor unions joined the AMA in opposing the bill, which they felt was not comprehensive enough. During his reelection campaign in 1972, Nixon blasted Democrats in Congress for not moving a health care bill through Congress, much as Truman did to Republicans in 1948.

Finally, after decades of effort, the Affordable Care Act (ACA) was passed in 2010. It was a formidable bill, but its architects seem to have come to terms with the many veto opportunities that would be exploited by the determined opposition. The bill shored up the private insurance industry, limited its application to companies with at least fifty employees, required an individual mandate but no public option, and doubled down on federalism by expanding health care coverage through state Medicaid programs. This latter point proved to be the Achilles heel when the Supreme Court declared Medicaid expansion an unconstitutional exercise of Congress's spending power. As a result, many Americans who would have been covered by the bill were left out.

Americans understand that the political system is unfairly dominated by elites, and they have long resisted the idea that those with the most economic and political power should control national policy. This applies to older titans of railroad, coal, oil, and steel industries and newer concentrated forms of wealth like pharmaceuticals, health insurance companies, real estate magnates, and tech giants. The conventional wisdom's abstract appeal to the interests of political minorities completely obscures the fact that it is *powerful* minorities, more than vulnerable ones, that have the greatest access to checkpoints.

A final and particularly pernicious flaw in the conventional checks and balances wisdom is that the fixation on restraining government obscures the crucial role of the public in demanding policy action in the public interest. Some blame the fact that Republicans control both the White House and Congress for why traditional checks and balances aren't working. But unified government is important for getting government to do the work that the people want it to do. Over the past century, many if not most of the major policy enactments that Americans generally want to protect or even expand—like Social Security and Medicare, minimum wage, labor organizing, and civil rights—were enacted during the New Deal and Great Society, when one party *decisively* controlled both the legislative and executive branches *and* responded to broad social movements and public demand for change.

This is another reason why simply calling for congressional checks on Trump without tying them to a positive governmental agenda is a limited strategy. The problem is not that Republicans in Congress are acquiescing to the president's actions. The problem is the substance of the president's actions, which are self-dealing, undemocratic, authoritarian, dangerous to democratic foundations (including due process, free speech, free press, and impartial courts), and antithetical to the economic uplift of working Americans he pledged on the campaign trail. Abstract appeals to checking the president without a clearer vision of what government *should* do risks reinforcing the same old narrative that powerful political minorities use against presidents genuinely trying to produce effective public policy.

Indeed, while checks on government are essential to constraining the dangers of arbitrary power, we rarely think about mass politics as one such check. Quite the contrary: some political appeals to checks and balances suggest that dangerously misinformed and morally backward mass publics are the primary drivers of authoritarianism, while more responsible elite institutions must work to keep them in check. On this view, the majority of the American people themselves are the problem, and GOP elites today are simply responding to them.

In reality, the rise of Trump in the Republican Party owes a great deal to the unresponsive Republican establishment, not only at the national but also local level. Decades of GOP policies in Republican-led states led to poor economic outcomes for the many and growing wealth for the few. Low taxes, federal income transfers, and military bases helped keep states like Louisiana, Oklahoma, and South Dakota stable for decades. But when free trade and globalization upended this system, Republican lawmakers in many of these states only made matters worse. Instead of investing in hospitals, universities, and public infrastructure, they slashed public services and adopted increasingly aggressive anti-regulatory, anti-tax policies. This state of affairs proved fertile ground for extremism among rank-and-file Republicans. Party leaders not only opened the door to Trump; they failed to understand the breadth and depth of resentment he tapped into.

Democrats, for their part, largely wrote off these voters, embraced some of the same economic policies as Republicans, and then failed to understand that the wider frustration with elite governance and institutional inertia applied to them as well. While conservative elites spent decades masking powerful economic interests as vulnerable political minorities, liberal elites contributed to the majority tyranny myth by assuming that college-educated elites know more about the needs of the people better than the people themselves. If we are keeping a ledger of anti-democratic behavior, we must account for the self-dealing and repressive actions of elites, who are more often the ones breaking democratic norms and institutions. As political scientist Larry Bartels puts it, "democracy erodes from the top."

From universal health care to a higher minimum wage, popular reforms are vetoed again and again by elites.

Tempering extremism in the United States therefore requires constraining elites more than constraining majorities. The checks and balances narrative paints the government as a perennial danger to the public and opponents as engaged in heroic struggles to check its overreach. In reality, it is often the other way around: government action could protect the public from the dangers of concentrated private power, but elites exploit our complex system of checks and balances to block it.

WHERE DO WE GO from here?

Many paths are open, none of them easy or assured. Some have looked to American federalism itself as a source of resistance to Trump's abuses of power and a bulwark against creeping authoritarianism. The day after the election, California Governor Gavin Newsom declared his intent to "stand with states across our nation to defend our Constitution and uphold the rule of law." "Federalism is the cornerstone of our democracy," he added. "It's the United STATES of America." Meanwhile, some scholars have noted that, given the country's deeply decentralized decision-making on core government functions, such as state courts, elections officials, and law enforcement, it would be difficult for the Trump administration to commandeer all of these institutions in a majority of American states, let alone all fifty.

That is probably true. But if Americans champion these arrangements, they should not do so by embracing the constitutional authority of state governments, itself an obstacle to effective governance. The fact is that American-style federalism has long served as a veto of the national public interest by allowing for legal challenges against duly enacted national policy in the public interest and by facilitating state-level variation (and hence inequality) in government standards and effectiveness.

The brutal history of racial subjugation is the starkest example. As far back as the 1840s, powerful plantation enslavers made forceful constitutional arguments for the rights of slaveholding states to exercise a veto on the national government when questions of slavery were at stake. This argument about state power persisted, even after the Civil War amendments plainly ended any such constitutional claims, and the virtues of federalism and states' rights became central to white segregationists' political and legal efforts to protect racial hierarchy. The power of white Southerners in Congress provided a formidable obstacle to national voting rights enforcement and anti-lynching legislation, for example, which left Black Americans exposed to lawless violence and repression.

The major aim of the radical Republicans after the Civil War was to alter the Constitution so that national authority would prevail over Southern elites who monopolized power with an iron fist. After the Fifteenth Amendment barred states from abridging the right to vote on the basis of race, it took a century of tireless and dangerous work on the part of dedicated civil rights activists to formally quash this power. Even then, national nondiscrimination rules and enforcement were repeatedly killed off by checks and balances, often in the Senate, where malapportionment and the filibuster give Senators representing a minority of Americans disproportionate power. In 1966, for example, an effort to amend the 1964 Civil Rights Act to bar discrimination in the sale and rental of housing fell prey to a Senate minority. After passing the House, the Senate failed to end a filibuster with a 54–42 vote—a majority, but short of the two-thirds supermajority to overcome a filibuster then required by cloture. By this point, some northern Republicans, who had been champions of equality under the law, were already shifting course; the filibuster was led by Everett Dirksen from Illinois.

Federalism also plays a significant role in deep geographical dis-parities in health and economic outcomes more broadly, which in turn contribute to the persistence of material racial inequality. The rallying cry to devolve constitutional authority to states and municipalities as-sumes that smaller constituencies are less susceptible to private, elite dominance than larger ones. But power asymmetries may be even worse at the local level. Moreover, appeals to local policy preferences obscure the many economic experiences and preferences that Americans have in common, like a living wage, public safety, affordable housing, quality public education, and so on. Abstractly reinforcing the veto features of federalism, then, won't generate more democratic accountability in the long run.

A more promising strategy is to make constitutional reform a public priority by acknowledging the wide gap between our political institu-tions and genuine democratic accountability. There are ways to do this without tearing down the Constitution or the Framers. Older traditions that articulated demands in terms of anti-oligarchy, equality of the law, and social progress all have constitutional roots. However unlikely constitutional change is the short term, this is exactly the right time to put amendments and statutory reforms on the agenda that could expand public pressure on elites, such as passing a national voting rights bill, limiting gerrymandering, eliminating the Electoral College and ensuring a majority vote for the winner, amending lifetime appointments for fed-eral judges, reducing the power of the Senate in national policymaking (perhaps as a body that can delay but not veto), expanding the House of Representatives to better represent the people, giving Congress the power to regulate money in elections, and clarifying the scope of execu-tive power—to name just a few.

But such reforms must be part of a larger vision that seeks to open the political system to the interests of ordinary Americans. If these re-forms seem likely to fall prey to the very veto points they are trying to overcome, how about a constitutional amendment that gives regular people a constitutional role, such as citizens' assemblies with a direct voice in Congress? The heads of political parties, interest groups, lob-bying firms, business organizations, and other elites across the upper echelons of the income ladder might react with horror to such a proposal. That they would feel free to publicly express this view speaks volumes about how little we think of the ability of mass publics to play more of a role in establishing the rules that govern us all.

Working out the details of these and other proposals—and developing the power to advocate for them—will not happen overnight. But we must not resign ourselves to the idea that we are destined to live with our broken system forever. In fact, nearly all of the substantive amendments to the Constitution since the Eleventh in 1795 have made it more inclusive, more democratic, or sought to strengthen the national government and make it more effective. It took forty-two years from the time women's suffrage was first introduced in Congress until its ratification in 1920. Constitutional change has happened before, and it can happen again.

The key to rescuing American politics isn't embracing restraints on government but mobilizing majorities around the needs of ordinary people.

The key to this and indeed any other strategy for rescuing American politics is to pursue the only remedy with a track record of overcoming the juggernaut of American veto points: mobilizing mass majorities on the basis of responsiveness to ordinary people's needs. There is simply no substitute for good, broad-based politics that recruits sufficient numbers of voters to the cause. Such movements are themselves democratic institutions. Mass publics already support economic and social policy reforms that would benefit the vast majority of Americans, including racial and ethnic minorities and low-income people.

One of the tragedies of the checks and balances narrative is that it gives the impression that mass majorities *routinely* pose great danger to marginalized political minorities—especially racial and sexual minorities. On the contrary, Americans today are broadly supportive of equal treatment under the law, protections against discrimination, fairness of economic opportunity and social policy provision, and even the diversity, equity, and inclusion initiatives that Trump has attacked so vigorously. Cross-racial organizing has a long and proud tradition in American politics, with substantial successes. Where these efforts fail, the problem in many cases arguably owes more to the country's excess of veto opportunities—and their effective use by an intense, elite white minority—than to majority preferences. By elevating extreme but minority positions, our deeply fragmented political structure has the effect of making it seem that Americans are more divided than they actually are.

The 1966 efforts to amend the Civil Rights Act and the failed health insurance bills of the twentieth century are cases in point. Trump's approach to governance so far is another: he has focused on bypassing the Republican-controlled Congress through executive orders not just to work quickly or "flood the zone," in the words of Steve Bannon, but to avoid failure, since much of his agenda is unpopular, even among Republicans. The complexity of American checks and balances provides many opportunities for organized and resourced opponents to empower parts rather than the whole. But savvy activists, organizers, and leaders of both political parties and social movements should consistently point this out for what it is: powerful actors resisting reform because it would reduce their power and influence.

A REVITALIZED, MASS DEMOCRATIC POLITICS that holds mainstream parties accountable has the potential to limit the ability of elites to monopolize power and neglect public need, as well as to constrain the extremists that threaten American democracy. Given the recent history of the GOP, the most promising avenue for such politics will be through the Democratic Party. Broadening the party's political power in a massive way will hardly be easy, given both the deep divisions between liberals and the left and the large number of Americans who have opted out of partisan politics altogether. But it is not unprecedented; most major reforms to American politics have been partisan *and* majoritarian.

U.S. history is filled with examples of political conflicts challenging the institutional status quo. Elite power was a major point of contestation in the early Republic and, in the form of plantation enslavers, a central cause of the Civil War. It animated Americans in the late nineteenth century as they pursued Reconstruction. It motivated some of the most important socioeconomic policies and democratizing moments of the twentieth century, from the labor movement and women's suffrage to the civil rights movement. And it has powered the revival of private-sector union organizing in this century. If Americans had a better understanding of this history—how American-style checks and balances really function, and Americans' repeated efforts to overcome them—a new vision of the constitutional system might gain traction.

The bottom line is that democracies depend not only on ensuring that the full demos can participate, but also on guaranteeing that political institutions have sufficient power for the demos to exercise influence over society's most entrenched and influential individuals and groups. Americans have been fighting for both since the ratification debates of the eighteenth century. It is imperative to recognize that this is the fight we now face once again. **BR**

Constitutional change is likeliest to come from big battles around basic needs.

Eric Blanc

RESPONSES

LISA MILLER'S case against the myth of American checks and balances is spot-on. In my corner of the world—organized labor—an overestimation of the power of the courts and an underestimation of mass politics have contributed to most union leaders' exasperatingly milquetoast response to Trumpism 2.0.

While it's good that unions have filed legal challenges to Trump and Musk's authoritarian wrecking-ball operation, it's remarkable that so few federal unions—to say nothing of the broader labor movement—have yet to really mobilize their ranks to fight back against this existential threat. What did labor officials do after Trump's executive order stripped a million federal workers of their collective bargaining? Call for widescale protests, disruptive sit-ins, workplace actions? No. They filed lawsuits and emailed their members to call Congress.

As I write, a judge has just issued a temporary injunction. But even if this legalistic approach holds and manages to slow down parts of MAGA's agenda, it seems far-fetched to expect a reactionary Supreme Court to ultimately safeguard our federal services or union rights. There's an urgent need for the labor movement as a whole to take its lead from efforts like the Federal Unionists Network, which has been pushing for mass action by workers and community members to save our services.

Where I think Miller's case could be clearer relates to the question of how we get a majority of working-class Americans to care about the constitutional reforms she justifiably champions. She is right to affirm that "the only remedy with a track record of overcoming the juggernaut of American veto points" is "mobilizing mass majorities on the basis of responsiveness to ordinary people's needs." Yet this assertion stands in tension with her subsequent suggestions that getting ordinary people to care about political reform is largely a question of political education—the idea that "if Americans had a better understanding of this history—how American-style checks and balances really function, and Americans' repeated efforts to overcome them—a new vision of the constitutional system might gain traction."

While I agree that it's useful to try to educate people about democratic deficiencies in our regime—as well as past fights for political reform—I'm skeptical that these efforts will make much headway on their own, separate from mass movements focused on addressing working people's immediate needs for economic security, affordable health care and housing, and a voice at work. It's hard enough to organize ordinary people around these day-to-day concerns; we shouldn't think that education alone will be enough to galvanize a mass movement for the seemingly more distant issue of constitutional change.

We've seen glimpses of what an alternative strategy can look like in the recent private sector labor uptick at Starbucks and beyond. Tens of thousands of young workers surged into action for better working conditions, fair pay, and an end to management despotism. But the experience of this fight itself—including being directly impacted by the limitations of a National Labor Relations Board (NLRB) deprived of strong powers to enforce union rights—quickly made labor law reform a relevant question for these young workers in motion. It was at only at that point, and as active participants in this movement, that organizers could start getting a wider hearing for the importance of reforming our legal system and fully funding the NLRB—issues that otherwise might have seemed somewhat arcane.

On a much wider scale, millions of workers supported President Roosevelt's push in the late 1930s to curb Supreme Court authority. Why? Because they wanted to cement their recent unionization breakthroughs and wage gains. And even then, the way public pressure ultimately helped persuade the Court to unexpectedly uphold the National Labor Relations Act was through militant sit-down strikes at Flint and beyond—actions squarely focused on economic dignity and workplace democracy. Though it would have been great to have seen a mass movement of working people emerge for broader political reform, constitutional questions only really became a question of progressive mass politics insofar as they were tied to more down-to-earth battles.

Things might look different if we had a mass labor party in the United States. In other countries, the emergence of working-class political institutions significantly raised the broader salience of political reform. Yet even in these cases, it often took a central focus on socioeconomic questions to capture the imagination of working people. German socialist feminist Clara Zetkin, for example, argued that the fight for universal suffrage could only root itself beyond upper- and middle-class circles if political transformation was framed primarily as a tool for *social* transformation. Abstract debates about principles could only go so far. As she put it, the movement would "need other grounds of action, other considerations, other ideals if the masses are ever to be reached."

Miller may in fact agree with these considerations; other elements of her argument suggest as much. But it's necessary to insist upon them since much of the Democratic Party and the anti-Trump opposition remains disproportionately middle class—and, not unrelatedly, excessively focused on high-level political questions. When you're not facing consistent material insecurity—when you're not one of the 60 percent of Americans living paycheck to paycheck—it's easy to downplay the issues that are most widely and deeply felt by working people.

My hunch is that our best bet for mobilizing working people against Musk and Trump's authoritarian power grab is through fights in defense of their Social Security and Medicaid benefits, the other essential services they depend on, their jobs, and their unions. If and when large numbers of workaday Americans eventually start demanding constitutional reform, this will likely emerge out of, and be in direct relationship to, big battles around their economic and social needs.

States offer the most realistic chance at progress.
Marcus Gadson

THE SYSTEM is not functioning well—Lisa Miller is right about that. She insightfully dissects the limits of our traditional understanding of checks and balances, showing why a major national movement to increase the influence of ordinary Americans is necessary. But as counterintuitive as it may sound, the best way to achieve the constitutional reforms we need is to focus advocacy on the state level.

Given her skepticism of "progressive federalism," Miller appears to think this approach is misguided. Indeed, when national politics consumes so much of our attention, an agenda centered on states may seem hopelessly inadequate. But hear me out. States have played a critical role in constructing the best parts of America's political order, and they offer the most realistic chance at progress.

First, history shows that states have been sites of our most important political innovations. When Thomas Jefferson wrote the Declaration of Independence, he drew heavily on Virginia's 1776 Declaration of Rights (later formally added to its constitution). Like other states, Virginia had already taken up the task of codifying who counted as Americans, how to structure government, and how to prevent tyranny. As ratified in 1788, the U.S. Constitution itself borrowed from these state constitutions—following Massachusetts's lead in giving the executive a veto and an independent power base, for instance. After a sharp outcry, the Bill of Rights was codified, adding guarantees to jury trials and religious liberty that Americans were already accustomed to seeing in their state constitutions. This is not to say that states got everything right; South Carolina's 1790 constitution, for example, made owning slaves one way to qualify for a seat in the state's House of Representatives. But essential steps in developing American democracy took place at the state level.

Important social movements first bore fruit at the state level, too. While the U.S. Constitution tolerated the slave trade until 1808, counted slaves as three-fifths of a person for purposes of representation, and required the return of fugitive slaves, Vermont abolished slavery in its first state constitution. Many other states did the same, either in the text of their state constitutions or by court decision, before the Civil War.

Moreover, states were responsible for extending voting rights to ever more people. At the founding, all states but one conditioned suffrage on property ownership, but they abandoned these requirements in the nineteenth century in the face of movements to extend the franchise. On the eve of the Civil War, and well before the Fifteenth

Amendment prohibiting racial discrimination in voting, five states allowed Black men to vote on the same terms as whites, while others allowed Black men to vote if they met certain conditions. Several states already gave women the right to vote before the U.S. Constitution guaranteed it in 1920.

Similar examples abound. Public schools developed almost entirely at the state level, and early state constitutions discussed them at length. Today, every state constitution provides for public education, but the Supreme Court still does not interpret the U.S. Constitution to make education a fundamental right. Life tenure for federal judges—which Miller suggests repealing—is another case in point. States, by and large, did this over a century ago. The overwhelming majority of states subject judges to some kind of popular election; forty-seven give state supreme court justices fixed terms instead of life tenure, and thirty-one impose mandatory retirement ages. Only one state—Rhode Island—does neither.

But history isn't the only reason to look to the states to make government more responsive to the people. There is also no other realistic path to reform in the foreseeable future.

Miller suggests amending the Constitution, and there are good reasons for considering it. But as she acknowledges, this path is surely impossible in the near term. Article V of the Constitution provides two paths for amendment: either two-thirds of both houses of Congress can propose an amendment and then three-quarters of states can ratify, or two-thirds of states can call a constitutional convention and then three-quarters of states can ratify its amendments. Both routes require clearing a very high bar. Even Antonin Scalia once complained—"It ought to be hard, but not that hard," he said, after calculating that as few as 2 percent of the population can block an amendment. This steep barrier is why even changes with broad popular support, like the Equal Rights Amendment, haven't made their way into the Constitution.

Hopes in the courts are also misplaced. The current Supreme Court is a far cry from the Warren Court of the mid-twentieth century, which interpreted the Constitution in creative ways to address many critical challenges. Instead, the Roberts Court has totally refused to police partisan gerrymandering, making it possible for political parties to draw districts entrenching themselves in power and giving them a veto over meaningful changes to the status quo. Only states have taken action to combat partisan gerrymandering recently. And indeed, states are the most promising arena to work for other much-needed reforms, while the federal government remains closed to change.

Miller is right that frustrated Americans sometimes agree on the desirability of policies that our political system refuses to provide. But she overestimates the opening this provides in national politics, because we are also intensely divided. Social media and demagoguing politicians amplify our differences instead of finding constructive ways to resolve them. Fundamental disagreements about identity are a large part of America's story and bedevil us today, as issues like abortion and birthright citizenship show.

The corrupting influence of money in politics only magnifies the problem. Candidates must raise millions of dollars to run for office—this spring's Wisconsin Supreme Court race alone saw over $100 million in spending. Time spent raising this money would be much better used to meet constituents, debate issues, or implement policies. Wealthy individuals giving large sums to promote particular candidates surely expect something in exchange for that money, and their preferences often don't align with those of ordinary Americans. Currently elected politicians lack the incentive to change this system—structured around partisanship and campaign spending—because they benefit from it.

Fortunately, many states provide a convenient mechanism to work around recalcitrant political establishments. Twenty-six states and the District of Columbia allow voters to use initiatives or referenda. In many cases, citizens can place a constitutional amendment or law equivalent to a statute on the ballot and enact it into law when a majority of them vote in favor. Fourteen states allow voters to call a constitutional convention when enough residents petition to do so.

In other words, many citizens have real options for solving our most pressing problems at the state level. And succeeding there will improve national politics, too. The more states commit to preventing partisan gerrymandering, the more Congress will fairly represent all Americans, since states are the ones drawing congressional maps. And working to make state governments more responsive to citizens—while addressing significant challenges in ways that bring residents from diverse political perspectives together—will allow more Americans to experience a thriving democracy, which in turn is likely to raise expectations of national politics and provide a significant impetus to change.

None of this is to suggest that states aren't also at risk for democratic backsliding. Indeed, some states have experienced total democratic collapse before. But given our political system's distinctive features, the most realistic path to giving more power to the people at the national level runs directly through the states.

We can't fight the right with top-down ideas and bottom-up foot soldiers.

Gianpaolo Baiocchi

LISA MILLER persuasively debunks the myth that "checks and balances" will stop democracy's demise. I'd put it even more simply: against a chainsaw, the icon of today's global far right, no institutional solution will work. The question is, what will?

"Mass politics" is the right kind of answer, but it needs spelling out. Miller's vision assumes a direct line from mass mobilization to institutional reform and then a responsive, more equitable democracy. Reducing the Senate's veto power, abolishing the Electoral College, introducing citizens' assemblies: all these changes might well help secure higher wages, gun control, and universal health care. But mass mobilization should not be just an instrumental means to achieve predetermined reforms; it's a source of creativity and energy in itself. It is hard to imagine constitutional reforms themselves gaining popular traction, and even harder to imagine they wouldn't be captured and coopted if they miraculously got approved. Appeals to mass politics in the abstract often overlook what movements really want and the agency they bring—the practices, ideas, and inspiration that have always been the true sources of democratic renewal and innovation.

Taking mass mobilization seriously starts with a sharper diagnosis of obstacles to solidarity. The biggest divide in this country is not between Republicans and Democrats, or even between urban and suburban voters. It's between those who are mourning democratic institutions and those who never believed them in the first place—which is to say, we need to name the gulf between those for whom institutions have by and large worked and those who have always been left out or oppressed by them. The former group can't believe authoritarianism is "happening here," and the latter, not at all surprised, thinks there's not much that can be done. The mourners can't see why any Black, Latino, or immigrant voters would choose Trump, but the skeptics lack a credible way forward.

This divide mirrors the predicament in much of the world, providing fertile ground for the far right. In Latin America and Europe, for example, social-democratic parties have moved steadily rightward in search of an elusive vital "center," only to see their base eroded by right-wing movements that aren't afraid to rage against the machine. The electorate must choose between the least bad option, and the far right at least *seems* to voice popular discontent and speak for some of the dispossessed. The center left's typical defensive posture—in favor of a system that has failed so many—only makes things worse. Addressing people's disaffection requires acknowledging realities that at first might appear to strengthen the right's case or undermine the opposition's credibility. After all, center-left parties can't condemn the influence of the wealthy in politics, the way real estate speculation has shaped housing policy, or the ills of free trade when they are as responsible for these things as anyone else.

To find a way out of this chokehold, we must look beyond establishment liberalism to models of successful resistance. The international far right has been busy learning from each other—Brazil's coup attempt on January 8, 2023, borrowed from the January 6 storming of the U.S. Capitol, while Trump takes cues from Javier Milei and Recep Erdoğan—and the left should do the same. Fortunately, there's no shortage of global models of movement-based politics that fight the right simultaneously on institutional terrains—including electoral politics and structural reforms—and in legal realms. These radically democratic and left-wing populisms are legitimately bottom-up, criticize the failure of institutions even while competing in them, and put the needs and concerns of the most excluded—unorganized workers, the landless and houseless, immigrants, indigenous people and people of color—at their center.

La France Insoumise, for example, has emerged as a vehicle for social movements on the left to combat the far-right nationalism of Le Pen. Its radically democratic platform calls for popular assemblies to rewrite the constitution, direct citizen engagement in policymaking, and workers' rights, all anchored in an anti-fascist and anti-xenophobic campaign. In similar fashion, Spain's Barcelona en Comú (Barcelona in Common), with the support of Podemos, has helped to contain the ultranationalism of Vox.

Latin America offers inspiration too. At thirty-eight, Juan Grabois, leader of the Movement of Excluded Workers in Argentina, helped the center-left Union for the Homeland coalition come within a hair's breadth of winning the 2023 presidential primary with a movement-led campaign centered on Pope Francis's slogan of "Tierra, Techo y Trabajo" (land, housing, and labor). In Chile, Gabriel Boric won the presidency in 2021 with a platform that included rewriting the constitution through popular assemblies—a demand raised by street protests that centered feminist mobilizations, indigenous movements, and unorganized workers. And in Colombia in 2022, where the electoral left has been virtually nonexistent in recent years, Gustavo Petro and Francia Márquez defeated the far-right regime. Their exciting campaign drew energy from urban social movements to develop an antiracist, feminist, ecological, and redistributive platform for creating new kinds of democratic institutions—for example, by integrating longstanding indigenous and Afro-Colombian forms of collective governance into national politics.

Perhaps the most dramatic victory was the social movement coalition that returned Lula to power in Brazil in late 2022. His opponent, the far right's Jair Bolsonaro, had accomplished little in his presidency in legislative terms, but via executive order he had weakened many of Brazil's institutions—its science and technology infrastructure, robust public health system, public universities, and environmental protections. He also criminalized dissent, sowing distrust and encouraging police violence. While Lula's Workers' Party had been increasingly at odds with social movements—which thought that the party had fallen short of its promises in past administrations—the grassroots mobilization against Brazil's far-right populism brought together working-class, student, feminist, indigenous, Afro-Brazilian, and environmental justice movements. The mobilization campaign was so successful that it drew movements long skeptical of electoral politics, including the MTST (a radical housing movement) and the MST (landless workers).

Lula immediately reversed some of Bolsonaro's measures attacking indigenous rights, environmental protections, and social programs, but he has not yet achieved the larger goals of reforming the political system itself or systematically addressing the country's housing shortages. This, of course, is the reality of national politics everywhere: transformative proposals are hard to bring to fruition, even with stunning electoral victories. But to keep fighting, it's crucial that the movements that propel new leaders to power maintain their vitality and independence from the system even as they work to change it. This inside-outside strategy is the most important lesson of Lulism.

Is there any opening for such politics in the United States?

Bernie Sanders and AOC's recent anti-oligarchy barnstorming is an important start. They offer a truly transformative agenda, including a call for massive investment in social housing and building permanent organizing networks beyond electoral politics. In the same vein, Kshama Sawant's victories in the Seattle City Council have directly challenged neoliberal austerity and far-right populism, explicitly connecting movements around rent control, taxing Amazon, minimum wage increases, and policing. In New York, the Democratic Socialists of America has emerged as a significant electoral force, winning victories in city council and state assemblies while explicitly connecting street-level organizing around housing, policing, health care, and environmental justice to electoral strategy. The electrifying mayoral campaign of DSA member Zohran Mamdani has ignited left creativity. Rooted in movement organizing around tenant struggles, immigrants' rights, and racial justice, it offers a radically new policy platform while emphasizing deep community engagement and resisting the right's xenophobia.

There's no lack of social movement energy and creativity to draw on in the United States, from campus pro-Palestine protests to new union organizing and Land Back, food sovereignty, climate justice, and abolitionist movements. What we desperately need—not just to defeat the right, but to govern for all—are ways to translate those demands, ideas, and practices into institutional struggles. We can't fight authoritarianism with top-down ideas and bottom-up foot soldiers. We need a transformative project of popular power and radical democratic creativity, rooted in mass mobilization and sustained collective action.

To turn majoritarian dreams into reality, we must work with elites.
Samuel Moyn

THE HALLOWED STORY Americans like to tell about our constitutional order gets it precisely backward—on that, Lisa Miller is utterly convincing. Rather than empowering democracy, our system obstructs it with layer upon layer of veto points.

But the momentous problem is how to translate majority will into policy outcomes through institutions, and on this score Miller provides little guidance. A lot of people, arguably even a majority, have long thought that public policy should reflect majority sentiment with both greater success and fewer risks than under our current scheme. And yet here we are, with Donald Trump in office again and the liberal mythology of checks and balances as potent as ever. To turn majoritarian dreams into reality, it's clear that we advocates of majority rule and popular mobilization need a more robust theory of institutions, a different way of thinking about elites, and a political vision of the future that goes beyond merely reshaping our democratic mechanisms.

On the first point, the legislature is the traditional icon of democracy, so it might seem that our task should be to make Congress great again. The trouble is that no one knows how to do so. For the most part, legislators don't want power, not even within our heavily circumscribed constitutional order. A whole array of perverse incentives keeps them wary of forceful governance. As a result, elites across the partisan spectrum have colluded to render the American political regime far more presidential than it used to be, touting that office—and the vast system of administrative agencies it controls—for its greater effectiveness and speed. Miller's focus on the Affordable Care Act misses that its fate is more exception than rule. The last century of American political history is marked much more by the welcome embrace of an "unbound" executive, as Eric Posner and Adrian Vermeule put it, than by vaulting legislative ambition undone by courts or other checks.

None of this implies that the executive is the best vehicle for translating mass politics into majority rule. Many administrations before Trump show that the cure of presidentialism is often worse than the disease of legislative inaction. But if there is a better institution for channeling the mass politics that Miller rightly prizes, it has to be built or at least rebuilt. It is not just waiting in the wings on the other side of checks and balances, ready and willing to deliver majoritarianism if only our constitutional order had fewer veto points.

Second, this project will require a reckoning with the inevitability of elites, notwithstanding the danger they pose to democracy. Miller is absolutely right that the American order empowers elites to block the expression of majoritarian will. But for better or worse, the first lesson of modern political science is that oligarchy dies hard. I agree completely that it is a terrible look for elites—starting with our founders—to arrange that outcome. But elites aren't going anywhere any time soon, and if mass democracy is going to be elitist in some sense or other, then Plato's old dream of better elites is going to have to be our own.

It is true that the boundary between elites and masses can be shifted to spread power to more people. It is also true that we can try to make that boundary more rather than less permeable—what "meritocracy," now under much suspicion and rightly so, was supposed to achieve. Yet for all the love that participatory institutions like citizens' assemblies or juries may deserve, democrats also need to work harder to imagine and pursue desirable forms of elite administration and rule. Attacking checks and balances will do little to advance majority rule if it does not come with a substantial plan for organizing and collaborating with elites who will use their power to make policy responsive to majority opinion.

Finally, while so-called progressive federalism and court-centered legalism are indeed dead ends, any successful populism must subordinate matters of governance to matters of substance, both morally and strategically. The kind of country (and world) that Americans want is the most important matter. Calling for a politics of democratic empower-ment without a vision for what the power is for is like setting the table without a menu.

Miller thus gets it exactly right when she calls for a proactive po-litical agenda. She suggests what hers might be, from health care to the minimum wage. And she shows why majority rule and mass politics are not to be feared—in part because these things themselves can provide effective limits on power.

But abstract injunctions to revive politics are still a far cry from identifying what Americans should hope to achieve with democracy if they can get more of it. Without such clarity, hopes to democratize America might prove hostage to the lowering of expectations Miller rightly condemns—say, by leading us to set our sights on mere consti-tutional change. People rarely support changes in how they organize politics in the absence of promises of what a new politics will deliver. In critiquing the process obsessions of advocates of checks and balances, proposing new process is not enough.

It's only through an independent check that authoritarianism has ever been stopped.

Aziz Huq

LISA MILLER clearly comes to condemn Trump, not to praise him. Yet her polemic captures a common justification of his administration's vi-olent, cruel, and authoritarian ethnonationalism. This striking tension should raise questions about both her diagnosis of our democratic mal-aise and her prescription for solving it.

The stark contrast Miller draws—between a democracy-stulti-fying system of "checks and balances" and a majoritarian expression of popular will—is also central to the MAGA movement's rhetoric and actions. Echoing Trump's own language, Miller stresses that political institutions are "dominated by elites," leading to the "atrophy" of mass politics. Her invocation of "older traditions" of constitutional law, along with her call to mobilize "mass majorities" that respond to "ordinary people's needs," likewise echo the White House's proclamations of constitutional fidelity and its appeals to "ordinary Americans." And just as Miller decries the idea of states acting as "a veto of the national public interest," so the Trump administration has sued blue states over trans athlete and immigration policies it perceives as un-American.

Of course, it is possible that MAGA is right about the cause of our political dysfunction but wrong about what's to be done. Miller might distinguish her position from Trump's by arguing that her proposals, unlike his, are *actually* grounded in the interests and wishes of ordinary Americans. She does cite polls showing majority support for certain progressive policies. But Trump can point to more than hypothetical majorities. He secured an actual electoral victory by campaigning on very different issues than the ones Miller foregrounds. He won the popular vote in November by more than 2 million ballots thanks to substantial rightward shifts among "seemingly every possible grouping of Americans," as the *New York Times* put it. He won, moreover, without hiding his morally odious views or anti-democratic tendencies. And polling suggests that majorities still support some of his anti-immigrant and anti-trans policies, even after months of cruel crackdowns.

In short, it is hard to see how to embrace majoritarianism while condemning Trump's evisceration of equality, due process, and free speech. Some might view these hateful majoritarian sentiments as mere false consciousness, whipped up by a fractured media environment rife with misinformation. That may or may not be true—I am skeptical that online discourse, in particular, deserves as much blame as it often gets on this score—but it misses the point. Having made an argument grounded in actual politics, Miller must confront it in all its messiness. Appeals to an imagined, sanitized people won't do.

Since simple majoritarianism can't be the right remedy, we have reason to be skeptical of Miller's simple diagnosis: the specter she calls "checks and balances." Miller never precisely defines the term, but she takes aim at congressional committees, the federal courts, and the constitutional authority of the states. She suggests that these features of our system are by their nature counter-majoritarian and thus anathema to democracy. There is reason to be concerned about the difficulty of enacting progressive legislation in our presidentialist system, but Miller's argument paints with too broad a brush. Three considerations point to a more cautious position.

First, Miller treats Congress and the courts too rigidly, missing the many functions they perform. Congress does more than pass laws; it also acts as a "check" on lawless executive action through its investigative powers. The Senate's investigation of Trump's relations with Russia in his first term is a case in point: it exposed important information and shifted public opinion. To be sure, Congress's investigations can misfire or be misused. But if the goal is to resist oligarchy and make government work for ordinary Americans, shouldn't we welcome Congress's checking power on the presidency?

As for courts, Miller focuses on judicial review of legislation, which she appears to reject entirely. But courts, like Congress, play multiple roles. Besides reviewing laws, they adjudicate claims of individual rights against state violence and cruelty. In the first hundred days of Trump's second term, judicial intervention has been vital in slowing (if not completely stopping) the lawless abduction of noncitizens and citizens. Without judicial checks, it is safe to assume that far more horrific state violence would be carried out under the rubric of "immigration enforcement." Courts have also been pivotal in preventing the White House from lawlessly withholding federal funds from states and universities. No doubt Miller does not intend to embrace lawless authoritarianism. But she offers no framework for distinguishing essential "checks" from the ones she thinks should be jettisoned.

Second, "checks and balances" cannot play as large a role in our democratic dysfunction as Miller contends for the simple reason that bicameralism, congressional veto-gates, and judicial review were all present during the New Deal and the Great Society. Many other factors have contributed to this moment, including shifting coalitions within both national political parties; the changing strategies of capital in the face of diminishing returns from investment; and demographic shifts that have deepened partisan polarization. It is tempting to identify a lone villain, and Miller is absolutely right that wealthy elites exert far too much influence over public policy outcomes. But in an era when masked officers and unmarked vans are disappearing students in broad daylight, we need a more measured accounting of the goods, as well as bads, of stratified government power.

Finally, as Tom Ginsburg and I have argued, there is now a standard playbook for eroding democracy from within. The tried-and-true strategy is to aggregate power within the executive branch, disarming checks from the courts or legislatures. Once these checks are gone, elected autocrats tilt the electoral playing field so that opposition parties might still be able to participate in elections but stand little chance of winning. It's only thanks to the intervention of an independent check on the executive—say, a court or an autonomous election authority—that this process has ever been slowed or stopped.

For all these reasons, it's hard for me to see how abolishing checks and balances is what this moment calls for. We should reckon with oligarchy, but not by mounting a wholesale assault on the very institutions that do indeed serve as a safeguard against tyranny.

Faith in checks and balances stems from an even more dangerous faith in law and order.

Kelly Hayes & Maya Schenwar

As most of the federal government has declined to "check" the Trump administration over the past three months, a new imbalance has been established—one that favors the autocratic rule of a megalomaniac and the oligarchs who have purchased his favor. The failure of formal checks and balances to significantly stymie Trump is painfully clear. It is also not unprecedented. As Lisa Miller illustrates, checks and balances have been routinely weaponized to obstruct efforts to improve the lives of everyday people, maintaining a system of vast inequality in which policy favors the ultrawealthy.

We would only extend her argument by noting that faith in checks and balances tends to stem from an even more fundamental faith in "law and order." This faith too is misplaced, yet it is even more pernicious, since it justifies the government institutions responsible for two of the most spectacular and entrenched forms of inequality in the United States: policing and prisons. We agree that mass movements are the only real antidote to Trump's malevolence and the only path to true democracy. But tweaking our constitutional order without dismantling these inherently corrupt and unjust instruments used to enforce authoritarian rule will only leave the heart of our liberal fascist system intact. Checks and balances won't save us—and rule of law, as we know it, won't either.

The prison industrial complex is already a fully functioning system of disposal. It strips years from the lives of those it ensnares, who are forced to live in torturous conditions while the system's evils are largely rendered invisible. Fascist forces already have the means to cage and surveil massive numbers of people—and the infrastructure is expandable. Trump is currently seeking $45 billion to expand ICE jails. And as we have seen in recent months, local police can be deputized to unleash terror on immigrant communities.

Trump's abduction and incarceration of permanent residents and visa holders, including the political targeting of students like Rümeysa Öztürk and Mohsen Mahdawi and the disappearing of Kilmar Abrego Garcia, are certainly dire escalations. But the words of a plainclothes officer who participated in Oztürk's abduction—"We are not monsters.... We do what the government tells us"—should ring forebodingly in all of our ears. These kinds of actions are far more routine than most Americans are willing to admit. Trump may be particularly shameless and brazen in making a spectacle of authoritarian cruelty. But justified outrage should not keep us from seeing that his administration is not an absolute rupture from the past. On the contrary, Trump is sharply and rapidly intensifying the U.S. state's long and bipartisan history of abduction and caging, deploying these powerful, incredibly well-resourced instruments of repression for overtly fascist ends.

As anti-authoritarian thinker and strategist Scot Nakagawa has argued, "The expansion of America's carceral state since the 1970s is not solely about prisons and policing—it represents the exercise of power and control in service of the preservation of unjust and anti-democratic hierarchies." Just as neoliberalism encased markets— insulating capital from the impacts of labor organizing, government interventions, and the will of the people—so has the carceral state entrenched the norms of inequality. As the country's social safety nets have been slashed over the course of decades, huge investments have been made in police and prisons. Nearly 2 million people are incarcerated in the United States—more than any other country in the world—and almost half a million are confined by electronic shackles. Upon release, they are saddled with even deeper poverty. Even social services, educational systems, health care, and other forms of state-sponsored support are now pervaded by policing and surveillance.

From the criminalization of poverty, homelessness, and acts of survival and despair to the incessant targeting of social movements, prisons and policing have suppressed challenges to the system as the rich amassed obscene concentrations of wealth. The first U.S. police departments grew out of slave patrols, anti-immigrant vitriol, and the suppression of labor organizing, and that legacy—the protection of property and hierarchy at all costs—continues. While working-class people have faced increased precarity and uncertainty, an order ensuring stability at the top and immiseration for the rest has been violently maintained.

The result, as Andrew Krinks has argued, is "mass devotion" to criminalization in the United States, leading even many exploited people to "put their faith in the pseudo-divine power of cops and cages to make safe, which is to say, to save, in the midst of the existentially threatening disorder that colonial racial capitalism itself creates." But a system that disposes of people and enforces inequality will never function in the service of our liberation.

Moreover, the fetishization of law and order as the foil to fascism falls flat when so many of the U.S. government's deadly injustices are legal, from routine deportations to mass incarceration to military "aid." Condemning Trump and his ilk as "felons" and "lawbreakers" is not just the mirror image of Trump's characterization of immigrants and student protesters as gang members and terrorists. It lends credibility to a thoroughly unjust regime of punishment while dehumanizing people caged in our prisons and betraying those whose efforts to survive, self-determine, care for themselves, or act in opposition to fascist edicts will render them "criminals."

This is not to say that law has no role to play in resistance. It is crucial to use every tool at our disposal to defend against fascism, and that sometimes means engaging with the legal system through defense work, class action lawsuits, and legislative advocacy. The important work of organizations like the National Lawyers Guild, Palestine Legal, Movement Law Lab, Transgender Law Center, Just Futures Law, Transformative Justice Law Project, and many more remind us that dismantling death-making systems must include reducing immediate harms to human beings and communities. But engaging with the law in order to mitigate harm and change policy is a very different project from the "rule of law" reverence that goes hand in hand with criminalization and policing.

Rather than catering to that mythology, we must dismantle the lie that criminalization safeguards democracy and ensures our safety. The death-making potential of the public's faith in criminalization has now reached an inflection point. If we maintain our faith in these mechanisms of surveillance, control, stigmatization, and disposal, we are worshipping at the altar of our own destruction. We are faced with the ultimate surrender of our humanity, our freedom, and ourselves.

To mobilize people in mass opposition to fascism, bring forth a true social transformation, and usher in ways of living and governing ourselves that will not be conquered, bought, or co-opted by men like Musk and Trump, we need to embrace a truly liberatory vision. What decarceration, anti-deportation, and activist defense initiatives can we grow? What mutual aid efforts can we engage in? What community-building projects can we foster, to keep each other safe? What creative and journalistic endeavors can we undertake to inform and spark action? What radical shifts can we imagine that prioritize the redistribution of wealth and opportunity? What projects can we dream up to usher forth a future that leaves no one behind?

It's long past time to renounce the mass devotion to punishment, stigmatization, and disposal that helped create and continues to fuel this moment. In its stead, we need a movement of movements—a collaboration that recognizes our shared humanity and makes collective liberation its spiritual center.

We know how to win. The main obstacle is the Democratic Party.

Lily Geismer

THE DEMOCRATIC PARTY'S decision to double down on checks and balances as the best response to the Trump administration is only the latest reflection of its paucity of political vision. Both Joe Biden and Kamala Harris decried Trump as a dire threat to democracy last year—Harris going so far as to call him a fascist at a town hall in October—yet the Harris campaign did not offer a bold, transformative agenda equal to the reality of the moment.

For just one measure of this failure, look no further than the fact that nearly half of American adults lack adequate health insurance, yet the Democratic presidential candidate said virtually nothing of substance about health care during her campaign. Instead of presenting a program bold enough to compete with Trump's hateful politics of fear, Biden and Harris told voters that democracy was on the ballot.

Lisa Miller's devastating argument explains why this milquetoast proceduralism—masked as a campaign slogan and now governing strategy—was always doomed to fail. She recognizes Americans' disillusionment, rightly noting that they aren't interested in business as usual. She shows why courts can't substitute for politics, documenting how our constitutional system rewards the wealthy few at the expense of the many. And she rightly contends we do not have to reinvent the wheel when it comes to better political strategy. We have plenty of successful models. What's standing in the way is the modern Democratic Party itself.

Miller is less clear about the sources of this impasse, but here too the answer is not a mystery. The key problem is that the party has become utterly beholden to the professional class, not just in its electoral base but in its entire governing philosophy. Reviving the mass democratic politics that Miller rightly calls for will require breaking the iron grip that professional-class liberals—especially political consultants and strategists— maintain over the party's rhetoric, actions, and outlook.

This situation has a long history. From staffers and consultants to politicians themselves, people with professional training, especially in law and social science, began to dominate the party's ranks beginning in the 1960s. This background has suffused its whole sensibility. Going back at least to the Watergate Babies and extending through the Clinton, Obama, and Biden years, fealty to legal norms and procedural reforms has driven the party's pursuit of technocratic, small-bore solutions to crises in the economy and democracy itself. This is a sharp contrast from the version of bold New Deal politics that Miller evokes.

This approach hasn't stopped Democrats from winning elections and capturing the presidency over the past fifty years. But, especially recently, they have done so primarily by stressing how bad Republicans are, not by offering and delivering an ambitious agenda of their own. When they do wield power, they are always wary of going too far or looking too radical—too much, say, like Bernie Sanders. From Cass Sunstein's paeans to cost-benefit analysis and "nudging" to Obama's tepid pragmatism, the vague promise of hope and change is always subordinated to incrementalist faith in the system and the supposed virtues of bipartisan compromise. However different it seemed to some, Biden's late-stage bid to break with the neoliberal economic policies of his predecessors was too little, too late, ultimately succumbing to the same constrained politics. The pattern is stark: while Democrats have stubbornly hewed to professional-class respectability, the GOP has grown more and more extreme—courting ever more voters who used to vote blue while doing so.

It's not just the party's vision that has narrowed as a result; its electoral coalition has too. The liberal and left factions in the party have grown further apart, and it has come to rely ever more on affluent suburbs and dense urban centers—losing a broad base of support throughout the country.

Despite Biden and Harris's campaign messaging in 2024, professional-class liberals have shown a longstanding anxiety about populism and mass democracy. Writing off huge segments of society, they have adopted ever more complex strategies for "sculpting the electorate," as historian Julilly Kohler-Hausmann puts it. The rise of a new class of data-oriented campaign staffers and strategists in the 1990s played a critical role in shifting Democrats' electoral outreach away from the multiracial working class as a whole to hyper-targeted groups of swing voters. The effect has been to give up on trying to mobilize new constituencies, particularly from underrepresented groups—exactly what New Democrat strategists William Galston and Elaine Kamarck called for in the early years of the Democratic Leadership Council.

All the while, tactics like polling, focus-grouping, and direct-mail and email outreach have focused on identifying and connecting with voters as individuals. This approach might have short-term political benefits, but it is directly at odds with building the organized collectives required for mass mobilization. Moving away from it is essential to achieving the kind of fundamental change and mobilization that Miller calls for.

It's also essential for any hope of structural reform, since the only road to constitutional change runs through states that are not Democratic bastions. Yet over the last thirty years, professional-class politicians and operatives have pushed the Democratic Party to abandon much of the country, concentrating money and messaging on a few swing states in presidential and congressional races. During his tenure as chair of the Democratic National Committee between 2005 and 2009, Howard Dean tried to stem this tide, proposing that the party adopt a fifty-state strategy. Rahm Emanuel, Chuck Schumer, and their allies sharply dismissed the idea, which strategist Paul Begala famously derided as "hiring a bunch of staff people to wander around Utah and Mississippi and pick their nose." The critics won: since then, the party's outreach to "red" regions has only eroded further. But it's precisely this small-bore, elitist attitude that has to go.

There are signs that party leaders might finally be learning this lesson as they come to terms with their colossal loss in November. As I write, the Democratic National Committee has announced plans to boost funding to every state across the country. That is a step in the right direction, but it is just the beginning of the much larger populist correction the party needs to make in order to break the professional-class stranglehold.

That means articulating and following through on a transformative vision, not serving up another tepid defense of the system. It means creating infrastructure and launching mobilization campaigns in places like Utah and Mississippi, not just Pennsylvania and Wisconsin. It means building a more expansive and durable coalition rather than trying to engineer razor-thin victories with microtargeted appeals during election season. And it means connecting with ordinary people and changing policy at the state and local levels, not just gaming a narrative every four years to win the presidency.

Avoiding despotism must start well before we turn to courts as a last line of defense.

Lisa L. Miller replies:

I AM grateful for these provocative and engaging responses. Start with the elephant in the room: Is this the right moment to critique our system of checks and balances, after a near-majority of voters chose a man who stated he would only be a dictator "on day one"? Aziz Huq warns that too much criticism will likely play into Trump's hands since checks and balances are the "only" option for restraining authoritarianism.

But the question is not whether courts or legislative action can help—as vital democratic institutions they most certainly could, though it remains an open question whether they will. Rather, the question is whether a system that routinely inhibits the public from checking the power of both public and private elites can steer us toward a more democratic future. I think that is *exactly* the question we should be asking at this dire moment, at least if we are serious about democracy.

The mythology that has grown up around our constitutional order—almost a kind of civic religion—offers few clear assessments of how well it actually lives up to its promise to represent the will of the people, protect vulnerable minorities, and avoid despotism. Huq is understandably focused on the last of these functions, but it is not as separable from the others as he appears to think. Powerful elite minorities helped propel Trump to power, and we can expect they will continue to elevate autocrats—and others who threaten vulnerable minorities—if we do not constrain their power and influence. Avoiding despotism, that is, must start well before we turn to courts or congressional investigations as a last line of defense. It requires expanding democracy, which in turn requires acknowledging how American-style checks and balances severely obstruct the will of the people.

Huq concedes that our presidential system makes it difficult to enact legislation, but the requirement that three separately elected branches of government must agree in order to pass policy reform is only the tip of the iceberg. Our unusually complex system also includes the deeply malapportioned Senate (plus a particularly undemocratic filibuster), a counter-majoritarian Electoral College, a strong tradition of judicial supremacy overriding national legislation, and fifty state governments that often implement national policy in uneven ways, if they do so at all. It's not any one of these institutions but the sheer volume of veto opportunities that makes the United States unique in the democratic world, facilitating the extraordinary power of elites.

Yet it is precisely this plethora of checks that the prevailing narrative lauds for keeping concentrated power at bay. There is little place for mass publics in American-style checks and balances rhetoric, except as an object of derision. The same attitude is evident in Huq's exaggerated pessimism about the American people. Trump has now run three successive presidential campaigns and lost the popular vote in two of them. He won in November with less than a majority and a margin of victory of only 1.5 percentage points. And his polling numbers are the worst of any president since polling began. More importantly, electoral outcomes are not set in stone. There is no good reason to think that better politics can't mobilize a significant majority behind a very different vision for America, though Huq clarifies the profound skepticism of popular rule that leads so many to doubt that such a world is possible.

Samuel Moyn points out that elites are important to the mission of producing a more democratically responsive system. Indeed, elites in legislative and judicial bodies as well as social and economic institutions have always been a part of successful mass movements. We may indeed need "better elites" than, say, the professional class of technocrats that Lily Geismer sees at the head of the Democratic Party.

But, as Gianpaolo Baiocchi notes, effective social movements are not just aimed at predetermined outcomes, which elites too often choose. Rather, as I argued, movements are themselves democratic institutions and thus a source of creativity and energy in their own right. Eric Blanc also makes this point in relation to the labor movement, where "the experience of the fight itself" is a mechanism to empower ordinary people. The same is true of civil rights movements, both past and present. It's not clear how we get "better elites" without strong and sustained bottom-up mobilization and a direct challenge to the dominant checks and balances narrative, which contends that elites will check themselves.

Blanc also notes that movements are not built on abstract appeals to institutional change, but rather through substantive appeals: saving Social Security and Medicare, for example. I agree. Yet movements also need a constitutional vision, and reformers need to be prepared to confront the standard defenses of American-style checks and balances if they are to overcome them. This is part of my concern about appeals to federalism.

Marcus Gadson rightly calls attention to the vitality of state and local activism and reform in our extremely decentralized system—another way of seeing the significance of Geismer's call for a fifty-state strategy. But appeals to federalism have too often invoked state constitutional authority to defend elite power rather than to promote the public interest. That was the case in the twentieth century with legal challenges to national legislation on minimum wage and maximum hours, and it has been the case this century with the rejection of Medicaid expansion, voting rights, and gun safety policies. It's not enough to note that "states have played a critical role in constructing the best parts of America's political order." We must acknowledge that they have also played a critical role in constructing the worst. The unevenness of state policies is responsible for vast inequality of life expectancy, infant and maternal mortality, and premature death across the country. And some of the progress that states have made might have come from the national level in a less veto-prone national political system. Improving people's lives and promoting democratic institutions through state politics is a worthy goal, but it should be an interim one—always with an eye to achieving national policy floors.

In fact, it has primarily been periods of strong national authority that have produced dramatic progress in democratic institutions and better health and economic well-being. Huq wonders how American-style checks and balances can figure so prominently in our current malaise, given that they also existed during the New Deal and Great Society eras. The answer is the very majoritarianism that Huq decries. Thanks to powerful majority backing, those periods of U.S. history enjoyed an extremely rare alignment: unified government across all branches, staggering margins of victory by the president, and near supermajorities in Congress. Franklin D. Roosevelt won his presidential elections by an *average* of 14.9 percentage points. Lyndon Johnson won in 1964 by a margin of 22.6. And under both presidents, Democrats had 57 percent or more of the seats in both chambers (sometimes much more). Our government thus functioned more like a parliamentary system that was both partisan *and* popular. Policy and institutional change in the public interest occurred not because American-style checks and balances became "safeguards against tyranny" but because the thicket of veto points accessible to elites were finally overcome by the sheer magnitude of the political demand.

It is perhaps these challenges to democratic accountability that lead Kelly Hayes and Maya Schenwar to reject any reforms that remain situated within the U.S. legal order. If it is so hard to get even basic, popular policy reforms, how can we hope to ever eliminate the abusive institutions of American politics that characterize the carceral state? I am deeply sympathetic to their critique, but mass democracy rarely delivers radical change. That does not mean giving up on revolutionary visions—including abolition—but it does mean understanding that mass democratic politics, with all its messy attention to the day-to-day concerns of large majorities, imposes constraints on the timing and substance of what we can achieve.

Some of the earliest advocates of popular government saw it as a way to constrain the ability of wealthy citizens to dominate politics. Even Machiavelli understood that patricians seek to preserve or increase their dominance far more than ordinary people do. And unlike the masses, elites have both much to protect *and* greater access to power. As the late political scientist V. O. Key opined, "politics generally comes down, over the long run, to a conflict between those who have and those who have less." Democratic politics may be the only mechanism available to the have-nots for occasionally leveling the playing field. At a minimum, it should not further empower the haves—or legitimate their power with a misleading narrative. **BR**

THE NATIONAL SECURITY EXCEPTION

Debbie Nathan

A**N IMMIGRANT** to the United States with a green card walks into his apartment building. Homeland Security agents enter, handcuff him, whisk him into detention hundreds of miles away, and present him with papers for his removal from the country. Then the government makes a public statement: the man hasn't broken any laws, yet he's still deportable.

What is happening to former Columbia University student and Palestinian activist Mahmoud Khalil has rightly alarmed many Americans—as have subsequent arrests and deportations. Some have sought reassurance in the idea that since his abduction is nakedly unconstitutional, the institutions of American democracy—the Constitution, rule of law, brakes on the unchecked use of power—would swoop in to put an end to the madness. After all, we have the vaunted First Amendment. Surely his detention will prove legally frivolous.

And yet it hasn't. Yes, the First Amendment offers speech protections. But over a century of federal law has hogtied the judiciary—and most dramatically, the Supreme Court—when it comes to judges' ability to rule on the constitutionality of immigration rules. A lesser-known idea has also influenced congressional and executive branch-mandated immigration law for well over a century: the plenary power doctrine. According to the doctrine's principles, judges should avoid ruling on whether or not immigration laws are constitutional, even when it appears they are not. This exceptionalism is supposedly justified because immigration is tied to national sovereignty and security. With that logic, the plenary power doctrine has created a situation in which, as a legal scholar once noted, the mere mention of the word *immigration* "has been enough to propel the Court into a cataleptic trance."

The statute governing Khalil's detention derives from a section of immigration law that defines as deportable "an alien whose presence or activities in the United States the Secretary of State has reasonable ground to believe would have potentially serious adverse foreign policy consequences." Marco Rubio claims to have such grounds, appealing solely to Khalil's participation in Columbia protests of Israel's actions. Though the contention that these activities have "serious adverse foreign policy consequences" is laughable, an immigration judge has refused to rule on their constitutionality, and the case is already in higher courts. The question the judges will consider revolves around three crucial words in the statute: "foreign policy consequences."

As many have now noted, that language first appeared in the 1952 Immigration and Nationality Act (INA), an enormous body of immigration law that originated during the height of McCarthyism. More popularly known as the McCarran-Walter Act, some of its provisions were used to exclude and deport immigrants accused of being leftists, many of them Jews. (The law's coauthor, Pat McCarran, was a notorious antisemite.) Whenever the Department of Justice leveled the "Communist" or "Marxist" accusation as a reason for deportation, judges shrugged and said they could not rule on the case's constitutionality.

But understanding how this judicial powerlessness came about—and its dire implications for the protection of constitutional rights—requires going back still further in history.

———

IN THE UNITED STATES' first century, the federal government played little role in setting immigration policy: the Constitution contains no such enumerated power, and its management was left up to the states. As legal scholar Gerald L. Neuman notes in his book *Strangers to the Constitution*, even native-born Americans in the 1860s who relocated from one state to another were often called immigrants.

Then, in the 1870s, white politicians and white-dominated labor unions stoked a racist panic about Chinese laborers, who had started migrating en masse during the Gold Rush. The hysteria spurred Congress to pass the 1875 Page Act and the 1882 Chinese Exclusion Act, the first steps taken to federalize immigration policy. The doors were slammed shut to newcomers from China, but a large population of earlier arrivals became legal residents. Like green card holders today, they were permitted to leave temporarily. But in 1888, with anti-Chinese animus still at a fever pitch, Congress rescinded that permission with the Scott Act—leaving stranded many people who had gone to China to visit family.

Deportation might be "cruel," the Supreme Court wrote. But "any policy toward aliens," it continued, was to be "largely immune from judicial inquiry or interference."

One of them, Chae Chan Ping, was sailing back to San Francisco when the act took hold, unaware that his reentry permit had been canceled. Denied admittance, he sued the government, and his case reached the Supreme Court, which ruled against him. In its decision, the Court described the Chinese as "a menace to our civilization" and "an Oriental invasion." The United States needed to protect its sovereignty and security from danger, and decisions about how to combat the perils of immigration were now to be made solely by what the Court called "the legislative department."

But as immigration legal scholars Adam B. Cox and Cristina M. Rodríguez point out in their 2020 book, *The President and Immigration Law*, the legislative department encompassed both Congress and the executive—including, most importantly, the president. With those two branches in charge, the judiciary had no powers of review for constitutionality.

That abrogation marked the birth of the plenary power doctrine. Over subsequent years and cases, acceptance of the doctrine congealed into hard precedent, relied upon by both Congress and the executive branch in equal measure. As in Franklin Roosevelt's use of the Alien Enemies Act of 1798 during World War II to intern Americans into concentration camps—especially Japanese Americans—simply because of their ancestry, plenary power reasoning even bled into laws allowing the detention of U.S. citizens. The 1944 Supreme Court decision supporting internment, *Korematsu v. United States*, has since been roundly denounced by many Supreme Court justices but never formally overturned. Nor has the Court jettisoned *Korematsu*'s principle of unconditional judicial deference to the executive on national security matters.

Use of the doctrine reached its apex in the 1950s, when the government sought to deport noncitizens who had once been members of the Communist Party USA (itself banned by the 1954 Communist Control Act). Dora Coleman was one of them. A Jew born in Russia in 1900, she came to the United States as a thirteen-year-old and immediately went to work in Philadelphia sweatshops. While still a teen, she became a union organizer. In young adulthood, she was a sometime member of the Communist Party, joining intermittently when the organization responded to various social justice issues that Coleman sympathized with. By the 1940s she was married to a U.S. citizen, had three U.S.-born children, and owned a bric-a-brac shop in Philadelphia. In 1944 she applied to be naturalized. Six years later, the government had her in deportation proceedings.

The same happened to Robert Galvan, who immigrated to California from Mexico at age seven. By the 1940s he was a union activist at a tuna fish canning factory in San Diego. He was also a former member of the Communist Party—from back when it was legal and ran candidates for electoral office. Like Coleman, Galvan had a U.S. citizen spouse and children. And like Coleman, Galvan would find himself facing deportation.

The Supreme Court recurred to the plenary power doctrine to uphold deportation orders for both Coleman and Galvan. Coleman was one of three people whose cases were consolidated into one, *Harisiades v. Shaughnessy*. Deportation, the Court wrote in the 1952 decision, might be "unwise," even "cruel." But "any policy toward aliens," it continued, is so "vitally and intricately interwoven with contemporaneous policies in regard to the conduct of foreign relations, the war power, and the maintenance of a republican form of government . . . as to be largely immune from judicial inquiry or interference."

As for Galvan, the Supreme Court acknowledged in 1954 that what was being done to him could deprive someone "of all that makes life worth living." It could even constitute "banishment or exile." But even though, as Galvan's judges noted, deportation was comparable to the punishment suffered by people convicted of crimes, immigration law had few of the same due process rights as criminal law. Violating it was a mere administrative infraction, covered by civil law. What's more, immigration law had become so clotted by plenary power concepts that all the Court could say was that "we are not prepared to deem ourselves wiser or more sensitive to human rights than our predecessors."

Galvan was deported to Mexico. Coleman stayed in Philadelphia only because the Soviet Union would not take her back. In legal limbo, she had to periodically check in with immigration officers. A few years ago, I located her daughter, by then elderly. She told me her mother had lived in constant fear of being imprisoned on Ellis Island, which in the 1950s had a detention section for immigrants accused of Communism. Coleman died of a stroke in her early sixties; Galvan succumbed at forty-six.

MCCARTHYISM EVENTUALLY SPUTTERED OUT, and judicial acceptance of the plenary power doctrine began to lose some of its hold as law in general became more sensitive to human and civil rights and as judges broadened their application of due process on administrative and procedural grounds.

The evolution became apparent in some cases in lower courts. In 1995, Bill Clinton's administration tried to deport a Mexican government official, Mario Ruiz Massieu, who was wanted in Mexico on criminal charges. Ruiz Massieu was granted a visa to leave Mexico after his brother was assassinated, but after failing to declare all the cash in his possession at the Newark, New Jersey, airport, he was arrested and detained. In Ruiz Massieu's prosecution, U.S. Secretary of State Warren Christopher invoked a revised section of the INA originally created by the McCarran-Walter Act—essentially the same law Rubio is citing today. Christopher claimed that the United States was working to reform the Mexican justice system, and Ruiz Massieu's presence in the United States harmed that effort.

In New Jersey, a federal district court judge—in an odd twist of history, Maryanne Trump Barry, Donald Trump's sister—ruled in 1996 that this statute was unconstitutional. No one could obey it, Barry reasoned, since immigrants could never know if their presence in the United States would harm foreign policy interests, given that foreign policy is confidential and ever-changing. She questioned whether the judiciary should so easily defer to the other two branches of government at the expense of due process, challenging the plenary power doctrine head-on. Her decision was appealed and bumped down first to immigration court and then to the Board of Immigration Appeals, where judges ruled in 1999 that they had no authority to second-guess the secretary of state. Three months later, Ruiz Massieu committed suicide.

In 1996, Maryanne Trump Barry—Donald Trump's sister—ruled that the plenary power doctrine was unconstitutional.

Not long after the New Jersey ruling, another case, this time before the Supreme Court, frankly rejected the plenary power doctrine. It concerned Kim Ho Ma, a young immigrant who had committed crimes and was thus legally deportable. His case typified the skyrocketing of deportation orders against mostly young immigrant men, including green card holders, which began in 1996 under the Clinton administration—the year the government began routinely ousting noncitizens for convictions as minor as for shoplifting, even if those convictions, like Ma's, dated back years or decades.

Despite the government's attempts, Ma could not be returned to his native Cambodia: the country did not accept deportees. For years, the U.S. government had kept him and hundreds of other Cambodians locked up in indefinite immigration detention. In 1998 Ma filed a federal habeas corpus petition, arguing that his detention was unconstitutional. The Ninth Circuit rejected the plenary power doctrine and ruled for Ma in 2000. And then, the following year, the Supreme Court ruled in the related case *Zadvydas v. Davis* that immigration detention could generally not last past six months. Legal scholars celebrated, hoping for a new day for immigrants' civil rights.

That hope hit the wall of 9/11. In 2003 the Court ruled against another detained immigrant, Hyung Joon Kim, a Californian in his twenties who had arrived in the United States from South Korea as a young child. He had a green card, but he also had two criminal convictions from when he was a teenager—one for breaking and entering, another for shoplifting—that made him deportable. Pending deportation, he sought a hearing to release him, and by legal implication thousands of people like him, on bond.

In a 5-4 decision, the Court refused, citing the plenary power doctrine in so many words, just three years after it had rejected it in Ma's case. Writing for the majority, Chief Justice William Rehnquist stressed a ruling from almost three decades earlier, which noted that "in the exercise of its broad power over naturalization and immigration, Congress regularly makes rules that would be unacceptable if applied to citizens." Rehnquist went on to claim that Congress was "justifiably concerned" about crime committed by immigrants. With that ruling, plenary power was here to stay. Now, it was no longer acceptable to use it to advance starkly racist laws, but it could still excuse a host of civil rights violations—so long as they were executed in the name of "national security."

Fast-forward to Trump's first presidency. Days after his inauguration, he ordered a travel ban for people from seven countries, all with mainly Muslim populations. The executive order tracked language in the INA, which specifies that "whenever the President finds that the entry of any aliens or of any class of aliens into the United States would be detrimental to the interests of the United States, he may by proclamation, and for such period as he shall deem necessary, suspend the entry of all aliens or any class of aliens." At least one prominent Trump supporter favorably compared the ban to Japanese internment.

Almost immediately, the Muslim ban was challenged in lower courts as a violation of religious freedom. It was overturned as unconstitutional, based on evidence that Trump had exhibited frank animus toward Muslims: during his campaign, he had promised to create a database to track them and falsely claimed that thousands of them publicly cheered when the World Trade Center was bombed. The administration soon presented a cleaned-up version, however—one scrubbed of language that could be construed as animus but that still prohibited entry from mainly Muslim countries. In hearing the case for the new order, the Court again allowed that Trump had a history of anti-Muslim animus, but this time, a majority ruled that the judiciary could not closely scrutinize a law enacted by Congress or the executive if it claimed to protect national security. "The policy will be upheld," the Court wrote, "so long as it can reasonably be understood to result from a justification independent of unconstitutional grounds."

———————————

THAT IS THE WEIGHT of precedent we now face in Trump's second term, with his risible yet ominous claim that all pro-Palestine campus activists are antisemitic—despite the fact that quite a sizable proportion of them are Jews. The INA statute that Rubio has cited to justify Khalil's deportation seems wholly unmoored from reality.

Another problem Trump's targets face is that immigration courts aren't really courts, and the judges aren't really judges—at least, not as most Americans understand those terms. The judges are appointed by and directly answerable to the attorney general and under pressure to accede in their rulings to that office's fiat. That's because immigration courts are not—and never have been—part of the judiciary. In 1940 they were moved from the Department of Labor to the Department of Justice, implying that immigrants were dangerous people—invaders, Trump now says—from whom the country needed protection.

The first Trump administration cemented that ethos by politicizing the courts, imposing performance quotas on its judges in order to speed up deportations and hand-picking judges with backgrounds in prosecution and law enforcement. Not surprisingly, they are likelier to issue deportation orders than other judges. In addition, a study of immigration court case outcomes at the Board of Immigration Appeals published last year found numerous instances where judges "did not appear to understand the relevant legal principles, or applied them in a conclusory fashion, rather than engaging in a rigorous analysis based on the facts of the case and applicable law." And immigration courts make dramatically different rulings depending on where they are located. In the New York City system, judges affirm claims for asylum and other relief most of the time. In Louisiana, where Khalil and others have been held, the vast majority of judges issue denials a majority of the time.

Jamee Comans, who oversaw Khalil's case in April, is one of them. A former ICE attorney and before that a police officer, she said she would consider only whether Khalil could be removed from the United States under the statute cited by Rubio. "This court is without jurisdiction to entertain challenges to the validity of this law under the Constitution," she said as she delivered her ruling that Khalil was deportable. His attorneys said they were not surprised by the decision and would continue arguing in the immigration court system, as well as in a district court in New Jersey where Khalil has a habeas case pending. Ultimately, they may end up before the Supreme Court. Meanwhile, the plenary power doctrine continues to menace this country's entire judicial system, not to mention its democracy. **BR**

THE OUTCASTS OF ZION
Benjamin Balthaser

Being Jewish After the Destruction of Gaza: A Reckoning
Peter Beinart
Knopf, $26 (cloth)

The Threshold of Dissent: A History of American Jewish Critics of Zionism
Marjorie N. Feld
New York University Press, $30 (cloth)

Doppelganger: A Trip into the Mirror World
Naomi Klein
Farrar, Straus and Giroux, $30 (cloth)

Unsettled: American Jews and the Movement for Justice in Palestine
Oren Kroll-Zeldin
New York University Press, $30 (cloth)

Our Palestine Question: Israel and American Jewish Dissent, 1948–1978
Geoffrey Levin
Yale University Press, $38 (cloth)

THE YEAR BEFORE HIS death in 1967, Marxist and Holocaust refugee Isaac Deutscher was asked what defines a Jew. "Religion? I am an atheist," he replied, as the son of a Rabbi. "Jewish nationalism? I am an internationalist," he declared, as a famous critic of Zionism. He defined his Jewishness not by blood, soil, or god but by the intensity of his socialist commitments: the "force" of his "unconditional solidarity with the persecuted and exterminated."

Fifty years later, we are witnessing the first Jewish sovereign state since antiquity commit a genocide, backed by the full force of first the Biden administration and now Trump. Israel openly aligns with far-right, even fascist governments. Its leaders and organizations allied with the state work—with great effectiveness—to suppress dissent both within Israel and abroad, from Jews and non-Jews alike. And as all this unfolds, much of the institutional Jewish world, including organized religious groups, either applauds or stands mute. Except for notable exceptions in the United States, with Jewish Voice for Peace (JVP), Jews for Racial and Economic Justice (JFREJ) and IfNotNow (INN) leading dramatic sit-ins and building occupations, few if any legacy Jewish institutions have offered more than occasional handwringing at the scale of Palestinian suffering in Israel's ongoing war and apartheid. Indeed, in the name of protecting "Jewish safety," the well-resourced Anti-Defamation League—once a professed champion of civil rights—now backs armed raids of universities and makes excuses for Elon Musk's Nazi salutes, while the sole concern of the American Jewish Committee (AJC) is that Washington may not be supporting Israel enough.

While Deutscher came to reluctantly accept by the 1950s what appeared to be the inexorable fact of Israel's existence, he wrote in protest shortly after the 1967 Arab-Israeli War that Jews "should not allow even invocations of Auschwitz to blackmail us into supporting the wrong cause," noting that the real threat to Israel lay not in foreign armies but in the legitimate grievances of hundreds of thousands of displaced Palestinians. How did Deutscher's sentiments—once so prominent, even after 1948—become so sidelined in Jewish life? What made the force of Jewish identity so allied to reactionary and racialized state power?

Several recent books chronicling specifically American Jewish dissent from Zionism, past and present, demonstrate how this relatively recent Zionist "consensus" was manufactured. Geoffrey Levin and Marjorie N. Feld tell stories of once-mainstream dissidents and naysayers purged from the ranks of even straightforwardly liberal American Jewish institutions, demonstrating the force with which unconditional support for Israel had to be constructed from the top down in the immediate postwar era. Looking to the more recent past, Oren Kroll-Zeldin and Peter Beinart examine efforts—in Beinart's case, his own—to break through that heavily policed consensus since the turn of the century.

In a recent conversation with Beinart and Rachel Shabi for the *London Review of Books* podcast, Adam Shatz asked: Why bother, at this particular moment, to write about Jews? As I read through these narratives, it occurred to me that I was reading as much about the decline of American liberalism as about the transformation of American Jewish thought and institutions. As the contrast with Naomi Klein's recent memoir makes clear, none of these writers identifies as radical: on the contrary, their argument, more or less explicit, is that Jewish institutional life should live up to its long-held progressive values by applying to Israel the same liberal principles it applies to other areas of American politics. Can a group long associated with liberal causes—indeed, the group most identified with American liberalism, after African Americans—not only change its political valence, but dramatically reorient its exercise of political power?

Robert Loeb, executive of the 1970s American Jewish anti-occupation organization Breira, expressed the problem this way: Israeli attitudes toward Palestinians, he found, were in "direct contradiction to everything that I had been struggling for in the States in terms of civil rights." The perversity at the center of American Jewish liberalism is the fact that American liberalism's towering achievement, the end of Jim Crow, is precisely what Israel violates. Given the force of the Jewish identification with the American liberal tradition, engaging these histories can help us to ask whether there is anything in the liberal order that can be saved.

———

BOTH LEVIN AND FELD focus on American Jewish institutional history and its relationship to Zionism from the 1940s to the 1980s, between the Nakba and the Six-Day War. We can think of this period as a kind of interregnum when Zionism was not yet the consensus—indeed, when even major Jewish institutional figures offered stinging rebukes of Zionism and Israeli state policy in their official capacities as spokespeople for mainstream liberal Jewish organizations. As Feld and Levin tell it, the marginalization of such views can be narrated through three figures, metonyms perhaps for the Jewish whole: intellectuals and activists who represent broad and now only latent or exiled orientations, their fates demonstrating, as Matthew Berkman has framed it, how the "coercive consensus" came to be formed.

Levin's central figure is Don Peretz, an unlikely outcast of Zion. Born into a progressive Zionist family in 1922, he became the first Middle East advisor for the AJC, the largest and most important liberal Jewish organization in the United States. Founded in 1906, the group had two goals: to combat discrimination against American Jews and find coalitions with other like-minded liberal organizations such as the NAACP.

Founded at the turn of the century by mostly German-descended Jewish elites, it positioned itself as the guardian of Jewish respectability and assimilation, countering not only antisemites but also the working-class radicalism of newly immigrated Eastern and Southern European Jews.

As I read through these narratives of dissent, it occurred to me that I was reading as much about the decline of liberalism as the transformation of Jewish institutions.

As such, the AJC was initially ambivalent about Zionism. While welcoming the new Jewish state, the AJC also sought to remake Israel in its own image: a liberal democracy led by an educated, cosmopolitan bourgeoisie. Its early insistence on non-Zionism reflected an ambivalence based on suspicions of Jewish "particularism"—the fear that intense nationalist feeling among Zionists would threaten American Jewish assimilation and lead to charges of "dual loyalty." In addition, the AJC closely followed U.S. foreign policy: neither the Pentagon nor the newly emergent CIA were entirely sure yet about their new ally in the Middle East, nor how best to pursue its imperial interests in the region and with whom. A patriotic organization, the AJC squared its critical support for Zionism with its support for Truman and Eisenhower's anti-communism crusade at home and abroad.

Peretz was hired by the AJC in 1956 to consult, among other things, on a subject now out of bounds in polite Jewish society: the plight of over 700,000 Palestinian refugees of the 1948 war. As the AJC's magazine, *Commentary*, editorialized in 1951, "Jewish minds and consciences both in Israel and abroad have been troubled" by "an oppressed (and depressed) minority in the midst of a Jewish state." The author of the piece this note introduced, Judd Teller, quotes Palestinians who offered to be "good citizens of Israel" if they could return to their homes. "As Jews," AJC president Irving Engel later opined, "we know what lies behind the word 'refugee.'"

Peretz was clearly the man for the job. In January 1949, he had traveled to refugee camps and Palestinian villages that had been liquidated, organizing aid as a volunteer with the Quaker-affiliated American Friends Service Committee. What he encountered over the next eight months "deeply disturbed him," Levin relates. In a letter to the AJC's foreign affairs director, Peretz wrote that many Israelis "have an attitude toward the Arabs which resembles that of American 'racists,'" reminding his friend that fighting Jim Crow and other forms of discrimination is the very cause for which the AJC was ostensibly founded.

Peretz returned to the United States to start a doctorate at Columbia. After completing his dissertation in 1955—"the very first" on the Palestinian refugee crisis, Levin notes—the AJC promptly offered him a position, where he was soon at work producing a series of educational pamphlets. In these writings, Peretz cast doubt on Israel's claims—then as now—that Palestinians fled at the orders of Arab states and that refugees in toto refused to be citizens of a new Israeli state, provided they were guaranteed security and equal rights. While Peretz's work might strike readers today as even-handed, as he also criticizes Arab states for their antisemitic laws such as Jordan's ban on religious Jewish travelers, his views were too much for Israeli leaders and diplomats. Foreign Minister Golda Meir directed that a response be written documenting Israel's objections to one of Peretz's pamphlets. "It seems we should do more than we have previously to take this fellow out of the committee," an Israeli consul wrote, suggesting they try to tank his academic career. By 1958 he was out—the result of both direct intervention by Israel and actions by the executive board that did not reflect the wishes of AJC members.

The two other figures Feld and Levin chronicle may seem to be mirror opposites: the left-wing, Yiddish-speaking journalist William Zukerman and the Reform rabbi and head of the American Council for Judaism, Elmer Berger. Yet each illustrates how Zionism ran contrary to religious and secular common sense in the United States at mid-century.

Of the two, Berger had the greater impact. The first American Jewish group created specifically to oppose Zionism, the Council was founded in 1942 and initially expressed little concern with Palestinian oppression; its focus was rather a theological and even conservative argument regarding Jewish identity. Steeped in American Reform Judaism's late nineteenth-century "Pittsburgh Platform," the Council's Reform rabbis claimed that Jews constitute neither a secular people nor a nation but rather are defined by religious faith. Moreover, much like the AJC, the Council feared that Zionism would lead American Jews to be charged with "dual loyalty" and thwart assimilation. As with Reform Judaism's origins itself, the Council was far more anxious about Jewish extremism—religious, nationalist, or socialist—than it was about settler colonialism.

Both Levin and Feld chart how Rabbi Berger began to shift from a Jewish-centered, even reactionary critique of Zionism to one politically informed by the struggle for Palestinian rights and sovereignty. Central to this story is Berger's lifelong friendship with Palestinian scholar Fayez Sayegh, whom Berger met through their mutual work for American Friends of the Middle East (AFME). Berger's conversations and collaborations with Sayegh resulted in travels to the Middle East and connections with Palestinian nationalists abroad. Perhaps the highest-profile Palestinian to enter the American debate after the foundation of the state of Israel, Sayegh is most remembered today for his 1965 report *Zionist Colonialism in Palestine* and for helping to author the 1975 UN resolution declaring Zionism "a form of racism." Always careful to distinguish Zionism from Jewish people, Sayegh and Berger "found common ground" and "learned from the other," these books show. And much like Peretz, Berger saw "the squalor . . . the human degradation and above all, the eternal despair" of the Palestinian refugee camps firsthand, likening them to "camps in Germany where Jews lived." These experiences prompted Berger's political reorientation, away from Jewish self-interest and toward internationalist solidarity, through the late 1940s and into the 1950s.

The Council enjoyed a brief period of influence early in the Eisenhower administration, which led most materially to the U.S. State Department and even the CIA funding early fact-finding missions to Palestinian refugee camps. But it was targeted by the Israeli embassy as "a dangerous political foe" within the United States, Levin explains, and meanwhile its own internal divisions began to hamper its work with American Jews. At best indifferent or even hostile to the civil rights movement, and with an aging and bourgeois leadership, the Council was so moribund by the late 1960s that even the 1967 war and anti-imperial student protest could not revive its fortunes. While Berger went on to become, like Sayegh, an important spokesperson against Zionism, in some ways he moved far beyond the Council he had helped to found, creating his own anti-Zionist research organization and speaking once on stage with Stokely Carmichael in 1969 during a series of protests for Palestinian liberation at George Washington University.

Zukerman, for his part, is paradoxically the least well-known but culturally perhaps most recognizable of these three figures. He represented a once-dominant left wing Yiddishkeit sensibility, one that Levin associates with the Eastern European Jewish Workers Bund. Yet the Bund had very little presence in the United States—only a single office in New York City after the war, mostly catering to left-wing, Yiddish-speaking Holocaust refugees. Zukerman's political and cultural orientations—socialist and secular, culturally nationalist and yet anti-Zionist—owe less to the Bund than to the Popular Front of the 1930s, whose Jewish socialists and Communists took many similar positions as the Bund in a distinctly American context, supporting Soviet experiments in Jewish autonomous communities, Yiddish language, Jewish humanism—and of course, anti-Zionism. Zukerman, Feld summarizes, "saw the global, universal Jewish mission as one with socialism."

"It seems we should do more than we have previously to take this fellow out of the committee," an Israeli consul wrote.

While Zukerman never joined the Communist Party—and avoided blacklisting and prison during the Red Scare—he nonetheless identified Zionism with the forces of McCarthyism and racial apartheid. Writing for the newspaper he founded, the *Jewish Newsletter*, he compared the anti-Palestinian 1952 Israeli Citizenship Law to Jim Crow, drew a parallel between the permanent exile of Palestinians and the anticommunist and anti-immigrant McCarran-Walter Act, and likened Zionists to "Dixie-crats and the Ku-Klux-Klan." When Zukerman spoke of the "sacrifice of the principle of universal justice for reasons of nationalistic expediency," the analogy to American racism and Indian removal would not have been far from his left-wing readers' minds.

Zukerman spoke an idiom of an earlier socialist moment that embraced neither the Council's assimilationism nor the racially exclusive, militaristic nationalism of Zionism. In a 1934 essay for *The Nation*, he saw in early Zionists the "menace of Jewish fascism," noting with bitter irony that the "the newcomers [to Palestine] are not only the victims of fascism but spiritually also its supporters." Though he acknowledged many of the Jewish residents of Mandatory Palestine were themselves refugees from Europe, the most militant and successful of them, he decried, wanted "a fascism of their own" that, like European fascisms, wished to "revive the glory of their passing world." The idea of Zionism-as-fascism spoke not only to the racial violence inherent in the settler project but also to the ways that nation-building bound Jewish workers to the Jewish bourgeoisie. Referring to Zionism as "machine-gun Judaism," Zukerman linked the Jewish state to both gangsterism and militarism in a single image.

For a decade, the *Jewish Newsletter* became a hub of non- and anti-Zionist thinking; its board members included prominent left-wing Jewish intellectuals such as Erich Fromm and Rabbi Morris Lazaron as well gentile socialists such as Norm Thomas and Louis Nelson. According to Levin, writers in its pages discussed the Palestinian refugee issue "more consistently" than any other Jewish newspaper; it considered the question of Palestinian refugees as the "moral question" of its time. It was popular enough to appear in both college Hillels and Reform synagogues associated with the Council.

Yet it was also, in the end, mostly a one-man show. Its Yiddishkeit socialism did not reproduce itself in great enough numbers to fight the twin onslaughts of Jewish assimilation and increasingly compulsory Zionism. The *Newsletter* died with Zukerman in 1961; the collapse of the Council, and the AJC's formal adoption of support for Zionism as central to its mission in 1967, were further nails in its coffin. By the 1970s Jewish anti-Zionism would have no institutional home in America.

WHAT EXPLAINS JEWISH ANTI-ZIONISM'S resurgence today in groups like JVP, which has grown from a small group in the Bay Area in the late 1990s to a nationwide movement with tens of thousands of dues-paying members and dozens of active chapters across the country? I have often heard it said that American Jewish youth are more critical of Israel simply because they are further from the Holocaust — an explanation recently invoked by Joshua Leifer in *The Guardian*, suggesting the "intensity of the reaction" to Zionism among American Jews owes to the "proximity in time" to the death camps at Auschwitz and Buchenwald.

No doubt, distance from overt racism and bigotry shapes American Jewish attitudes, on a range of subjects. But it is a theoretical and historical error to conceive of Zionism as a necessary response to the horrors of antisemitism and the Judeocide of Europe, as prevailing Zionist narratives like to insist. The work of Levin and Feld expands our understanding of just how forcefully this consensus had to be manufactured in mainstream Jewish organizations. Norm Podhoretz famously asserted that American Jews "converted to Zionism" after 1973, but it was as much a conversion as coercion; the conservative forces of nationalism and assimilation into whiteness, not the trauma of the Holocaust, turned Jewish institutions into Zionist institutions. The Jewish protesters dropping banners reading "Never Again for Anyone" from Grand Central Station today exhibit a very different form of historical memory.

Two other recent books confront this present: Kroll-Zeldin's *Unsettled*, and Beinart's own *Being Jewish After the Destruction of Gaza*. They may seem to offer opposite, even irreconcilable, accounts—the one seeing a sort of vindication of American Jewish liberalism, and the other its enduring corruption.

Chronicling the rise of Jewish anti-Zionist movements over the last two decades, from JVP to INN and the Center for Jewish Nonviolence, Kroll-Zeldin sees an upswell of American Jewish liberalism against Israeli ethnonationalism and racial violence. Increasingly, he writes, Rabbis, students, and activists are "calling on the American Jewish community to consistently apply its liberal and progressive values to Israel." In the face of an Israeli state that repeatedly refused to make peace with Palestinians, engaged in ever-escalating and routine massacres, and elected far-right politicians, American Jews, Kroll-Zeldin argues, are choosing their liberalism over their Zionism. Citing Pew studies from 2020, *Unsettled* notes that for three-quarters of American Jews, caring about "being Jewish" remains "very" or "somewhat" important, while only 35 percent of American Jews under the age of thirty view "caring about Israel as essential to being Jewish," and a similar figure in that age range don't see Israel as important at all.

As Kroll-Zeldin makes clear, however, Jewish anti-Zionism did not merely emerge from within the American Jewish community. The end of the Second Intifada led many Palestinian intellectuals and activists to focus on nonviolent civil disobedience, including the Boycott, Divestment, and Sanctions campaign (BDS), which in turn provided space for American Jewish activists both to join in delegations to the West Bank to protect Palestinians from settler attacks and to help organize BDS movements in the United States in dialogue with Palestinian partners abroad. From occupying AIPAC offices to sitting in at Congress, holding die-ins in front of American businesses that trade with Israel to forming a critical and outsized constituency in the student-led encampments this past spring, anti-Zionist Jewish activism has taken an increasingly visible and pivotal role. Today, JVP—the most radical and one of the largest Jewish anti-Zionist organizations—grounds a parting of the ways over the meaning of Jewish identity in institutional, cultural, and political praxis.

Beinart sees things quite differently—not as a breaking apart of Israeli and American Jewish communities, old and young, right and left, as much as the corruption of a unified Jewish community, who all share in the blame and condemnation. Ironically, perhaps, Beinart is himself a sign of the rapidly changing American Jewish consensus on Israel. Once a liberal Zionist who supported the 2003 U.S. invasion of Iraq, Beinart broke with his Zionism, if not his liberalism, to advocate for an end to a Jewish-supremacist state in 2020, leaving *The Forward* to join the editorial team at anti-Zionist *Jewish Currents*.

Addressing his book to a former friend who still identifies as a Zionist, Beinart embraces the idea that Jews "are all each other's relatives." "I still believe in the metaphor of Jews as a family," he writes. After positing this still-coherent peoplehood, he makes his real target clear: the morality tales even liberal American Jews tell about Jewish history—that Jews are the world's eternal victims, and world history is the history of Jews surviving successive attempts to kill them. Where Kroll-Zeldin sees American liberalism as the fulcrum wrenching American Jews apart from Zionism, Beinart argues that this liberalism has a reactionary function: it is a balm in Gilead, a healing salve to reassure Jews that we are still the world's victims and can do no wrong. From narratives of antisemitism in which Jewish victimhood is deployed to silence critics of Israel to the Book of Esther and Deuteronomy, we mistake our new massacres for acts of self-defense. "Jews can be pharaohs too," Beinart warns.

But his prescription is not religious disenchantment. On the contrary, Beinart interprets the drive to Jewish nationhood in the Levant not as a consequence of European imperialism or a devil's bargain with Western antisemitism but as a result of the increased "secularization" of Jewish life. Rather than "describe ourselves as a people chosen by God to follow laws engraved at Sinai," he argues, we "describe ourselves as a people fated by history to perpetually face annihilation" only to "miraculously" survive. In evoking a cosmopolitan practice of religious commandment against the story of a people tied to land in a transhistorical quest for security, Beinart echoes scholar Shaul Magid's concept of an "exilic Judaism," which arose in full flower only after the destruction of the Second Temple by the Romans.

In this vision, reading Torah not only challenges the necessity of a state; it calls into question whether a state itself violates Jewish theology. As Magid frames the question, one can be in exile even in Jerusalem as long as one is not in accordance with the letter and spirit of Jewish law, which among other things holds the protection of human life as above all other values. While one might question Beinart's claim of Torah-as-refuge as itself a product of secularization—in the ancient world religion was very much an affair of the state, not a privatized escape from it—he is trying to answer a question very much on the minds of anti-Zionist Jews. After rejecting Zionism, to paraphrase a famous revolutionary song, how do we create a new world out of the ashes of the old?

Naomi Klein's *Doppelganger* is unique among these recent books in approaching the state of Jewish politics from the outside in: rather than ask how Jewish institutions became internally corrupted by Zionism, she traces the consolidation of Zionism into the mainstream through the rise of the global far right. *Doppelganger* suggests that fascism's rising appeal stems from cathexis with its other, the language and affect of the left. For Klein, Zionism is another "doppelganger" effect: just as anti-vaxxers position themselves as victims of state tyranny, the Jewish state appropriates the rhetoric of resistance to trauma and oppression, refashioning dreams of liberation into paranoid hyper-nationalism.

Klein is an outlier among these authors in another way, too: she neither writes from within the academic discipline of Jewish Studies, nor is she, like Beinart, a halachically observant Jew. The child of Jewish New Left war resisters who fled to Canada during the Vietnam War, she has made a name for herself as one of the primary chroniclers and spokespeople for a new post–Cold War left. Beginning with an analysis of the global justice movement, her books and wider writing have explained and defended movements against the Iraq War and neoliberalism and for climate justice. From this vantage, it makes sense that her account of her own anti-Zionism would emerge as less a dialectic within the Jewish world than of a piece with political movements for liberation. Her Jewishness—while something she has never been shy about—now seems called upon, if not by other Jews, then by history itself.

On this score, *Doppelganger*'s narrative runs not through American Jewish liberalism but global Jewish Marxism: Rosa Luxemburg, Walter Benjamin, Leon Trotsky, and Abram Leon. As her own background suggests, American Jewish anti-Zionism has far more often expressed itself outside of Jewish institutions than in, as evidenced by the outsized presence of American Jews in the radical left—from the Communist and socialist parties to Students for a Democratic Society and the Student Nonviolent Coordinating Committee. Throughout the twentieth century, Marxists opposed Zionism not on the grounds that it was a perversion of Jewish teachings and traditions but mainly on the basis that it was a right-wing nationalist tendency, in line with other forms of latent fascism.

Klein sees Zionism as another "doppelganger" effect: the Jewish state appropriates the rhetoric of the left, turning dreams of liberation into paranoid hyper-nationalism.

Citing Leon and Benjamin, Klein notes that fascism emerged as a countermovement to multi-ethnic working-class revolutions from Russia to Ireland, as well as to the stirrings of anticolonial revolt from Asia to the Middle East. The racialized trope of the "international Jew" was the scapegoat of the new socialist threat; the goal of fascism was always to eliminate Jewish alterity within Europe, by assimilation, expulsion, and finally genocide as a means to eliminate the left. With Israel, the fascists finally achieved their aim: to create a state and people in their own image, one that advances a global reactionary movement. Ascribing a mythic, timeless identity to Jewishness as the logic of a new "militarized ghetto" state is the apotheosis of fascism, not a resistance to it.

In this sense, Klein is able to synthesize the two theses of Beinart and Kroll-Zeldin: that Jews are simultaneously at the vanguard of contemporary fascism, and also, in the United States, behind some of the organizations most active in resisting it. One voice says Never Again for Jews; the other says Never Again for anyone. To put it in terms that Benjamin or Trotsky would approve of, Zionism is the form of today's class war against people's rebellions, and anti-Zionism its multi-ethnic, working-class antithesis. The Jew for Klein is thus the ultimate doppelganger, victim become victimizer, a figure that signifies histories of both Israeli state fascism and anti-fascism, colonizer and the internally colonized. Shylock, as Klein's reading of Philip Roth suggests, is the double here of Israel, the victim become victimizer, and the antisemitic image of the Jew forever bound by their wounding to wound. It is this slipperiness that gives the "anti-antisemitism" industry so much of its charge: it can persecute leftists in the very name of what was once a left-wing cause.

In this sense, the framework of "Jewish dissent" developed in the other books discussed here is far different from Klein's analysis—perhaps because of her relative distance from American Jewish institutional life, perhaps because of her different entry point of radical social movements, as opposed to ethnic or religious community. For Klein, while the figure of the dissenter is of course valuable, it is also rather fatalistic: a statement of individual principle, rather than the expression of global struggles to produce multi-ethnic, multiracial working-class majorities. At stake, she thinks, are not Jewish ethics or Jewish communal institutions so much as the ways that Jewish history, and popular Jewish movements in the past, can point to a collective future and provide historical footing for those who do wish to resist. Seen from this vantage, JVP is less a dissenting voice within an increasingly reactionary Jewish institutional world than a part of a new global majority rejecting colonialism, racial apartheid, and militarism.

WHILE KLEIN IS CLOSEST of these authors to my own personal genesis as an activist and writer—we both came of political age during the late 1990s "Battle of Seattle" and the rise of the first hemispheric, anticapitalist movement since the 1960s—I see all these books as an ensemble, part of a social formation still struggling to be born. They are all asking, more or less explicitly, whether the victories of twentieth-century social democracy we have come to take for granted—that all people deserve to have rights, that we all should have basic liberties to speak, protest, and receive care—can remain meaningfully universalist, both for those who benefitted from such reforms and those who did not.

And American Jews did indeed benefit. Once a marginalized, poor, and discriminated-against minority, they shot, in Grace Paley's words, "like a surface-to-air missile right into the middle class" after World War II. A result of mass unionization, the lifting of antisemitic quotas at universities and restrictive covenants in suburban housing, and state investment in public education and civil service, Jewish assimilation has long been held up as a sort of civic religion—proof that the United States is a liberal, welcoming, and increasingly inclusive society.

Jews themselves bought into this narrative en masse. They still vote Democratic as a group second only to African Americans—estimates show that around 70 percent voted for Kamala Harris in November—and they continue to support liberal issues such as abortion rights, gun control, and investments in public education at rates far higher than other American ethnic groups. It is as if American Jews are a kind of embodied memory of the successes of the New Deal and Great Society. Unlike Italian or Irish Americans, they still revere both the Civil Rights Act and Wagner Acts as crowning achievements of American liberal democracy. As my uncle was fond of saying, *the New Deal made us Americans.* It was not for nothing that reactionaries referred to the era of social and economic reform as the "Jew Deal."

But as Paley's image suggests, there is much this triumphant narrative conceals. American liberalism's greatest achievements, both before and after World War II, were as much a response to the threat of communism as they were a genuine commitment to fulfill the promises of social democracy; behind Kennedy and Johnson's visions stood Vietnam, as Martin Luther King Jr. famously invoked. In the decades since, American liberalism, in the form of the Democratic Party, has been complicit in mass incarceration, the expansion of the military-industrial complex, and the gutting of public goods and social services. Yet throughout all this, even as some Jews defected from civil rights to neoconservatism, the expectation prevailed that to be Jewish was, in some deep way, essentially to be liberal.

This may help to explain why Israel's genocide registers so sharply for so many Americans, even or especially American Jews: it is the final betrayal of American liberalism, in the most grotesque form imaginable. As historian Michelle Mart puts it, Israelis "became surrogate Americans." Both Israel and the United States are settler nations that consider themselves paradigms of the open society. From Leon Uris's novel *Exodus* (1958) to the lightning victories of the 1967 war, Israel was increasingly seen by Americans in the aftermath of the civil rights era as reviving the righteous idea of their own country after its defeat by Vietnamese guerrillas abroad and hippies and Black power at home. "There were no draft dodgers in Israel," historian Michael Fischbach writes of the late 1960s pro-Israel consensus—no Vietnam War, no burning ghettos, no drug addicts, no crime. Israel was Americans' Disneyland abroad, a fantasy of an ideal past long gone, which in reality never existed.

Legally and morally speaking, Jewish history formed the architecture for the liberal postwar order: from the Nuremburg trials to the UN's Geneva and Genocide Conventions, the new instruments of international law were all designed to prevent another Holocaust. As Pankaj Mishra has traced, Israel's genocide against Palestine functions as something more bitter than irony: the state to have emerged from the Shoah, indeed with that genocide as its raison d'être, commits the very crime such laws were intended to stop. And this is perhaps Israel's real horror: far from proving the "anachronism" that Deutscher described, it embodies the ethnonationalism of the future, beyond legal and moral restraints—a "portent," as Mishra writes, "of a bankrupt and exhausted world."

Can the United States, which framed its liberalism on a postwar order of human rights, live up to these values? It is not clear whether Jewish liberalism, to say nothing of a Jewish left, will arise triumphant from the ash heaps and killing fields of Zionism. Then again, it is not clear that the world will emerge from the rise of the far right and the entwined crises of wealth accumulation at one pole and immiseration at another, climate chaos, AI's new military-industrial complexes, and the expanding carceral state. To be sure, these are not the same question: Jews are a tiny minority worldwide, numerically roughly the population of Illinois.

Yet like the Jewish Question, Jews are bound up with the liberal story the West tells about itself. Whether American Jews manage to shed their Zionism may or may not decide whether the United States continues to support Israel, and thus whether Israel will be empowered to continue on its rampage of ethnic cleansing and war without end. Yet as these authors suggest, each in their own way, American Jews have a material stake in the outcome of a just future for Palestine and Palestinians that is tied as much to Israelis as it is whether or not the United States remains in any form the liberal democracy it promised to be post-1965. To this extent, parting ways with Zionism should also be seen as the condition of the rescue of American liberalism itself. **BR**

FROM THE ARCHIVE

ON POST-FASCISM

G. M. Tamás

From the Summer 2000 issue

This essay has unfortunately turned out to be one of the most prescient and insightful political texts of the new century. Writing in 2000, Tamás foresaw the emergence of a "post-totalitarian" variation on fascism that did not require street fighting, stormtroopers, the one-party state, or Führers but could instead nest itself in the structures of representative de-mocracy and the globalized economy to carry out its violently anti-Enlightenment project. That project was to roll back the universal expansion of citizenship—of the rights of man—and replace it with a narrower vision of national belonging based on race and ethnicity and to gradually turn domestic populations into foreign enemies. It is an essential text to understand our times, and Boston Review is among a shrinking few publications that would publish material of this seriousness and depth.

—John Ganz

I HAVE AN INTEREST to declare. The government of my country, Hungary, is—along with the Bavarian provincial government (provincial in more senses than one)—the strongest foreign supporter of Jörg Haider's Austria. The right-wing cabinet in Budapest, besides other misdeeds, is attempting to suppress parliamentary governance, penalizing local authorities of a different political hue than itself, and busily creating and imposing a novel state ideology, with the help of a number of *lumpen* intellectuals of the extreme right, including some overt neo-Nazis. It is in cahoots with an openly and viciously antisemitic fascistic party that is, alas, represented in parliament. People working for the prime minister's office are engaging in more or less cautious Holocaust revisionism. The government-controlled state television gives vent to raw anti-Gypsy racism. The fans of the most popular soccer club in the country, whose chairman is a cabinet minister and a party leader, are chanting in unison about the train that is bound to leave any moment for Auschwitz.

On the ground floor of the Central European University in Budapest you can visit an exhibition concerning the years of turmoil a decade or so ago. There you can watch a video recorded illegally in 1988, and you can see the current Hungarian prime minister defending and protecting me with his own body from the truncheons of communist riot police. Ten years later, this same person appointed a communist police general as his home secretary, the second or third most important person in the cabinet. Political conflicts between former friends and allies are usually acrimonious. This is no exception. I am an active participant in an incipient anti-fascist movement in Hungary, a speaker at rallies and demonstrations. Our opponents—in personal terms—are too close for comfort. Thus, I cannot consider myself a neutral observer.

The phenomenon that I shall call *post-fascism* is not unique to Central Europe. Far from it. To be sure, Germany, Austria, and Hungary are important, for historical reasons obvious to all; familiar phrases repeated here have different echoes. I recently saw that the old brick factory in Budapest's third district is being demolished; I am told that they will build a gated community of suburban villas in its place. The brick factory is where the Budapest Jews waited their turn to be transported to the concentration camps. You could as well build holiday cottages in Treblinka. Our vigilance in this part of the world is perhaps more needed than anywhere else, since innocence, in historical terms, cannot be presumed. Still, post-fascism is a cluster of policies, practices, routines, and ideologies that can be observed everywhere in the contemporary world; that have little or nothing to do, except in Central Europe, with the legacy of Nazism; that are not totalitarian; that are not at all revolutionary; and that are not based on violent mass movements and irrationalist, voluntaristic philosophies, nor are they toying, even in jest, with anti-capitalism.

Why call this cluster of phenomena *fascism*, however post-?

Post-fascism finds its niche easily in the new world of global capitalism without upsetting the dominant political forms of electoral democracy and representative government. It does what I consider to be central to all varieties of fascism, including the post-totalitarian version. *Sans* Führer, *sans* one-party rule, *sans* SA or SS, post-fascism *reverses the Enlightenment tendency to assimilate citizenship to the human condition.*

Before the Enlightenment, citizenship was a privilege, an elevated status limited by descent, class, race, creed, gender, political participation, morals, profession, patronage, and administrative fiat, not to speak of age and education. Active membership in the political community was a station to yearn for, *civis Romanus sum* the enunciation of a certain nobility. Policies extending citizenship may have been generous or stingy, but the rule was that the rank of citizen was conferred by the lawfully constituted authority, according to expediency. Christianity, like some Stoics, sought to transcend this kind of limited citizenship by considering it second-rate or inessential when compared to a virtual community of the saved. Freedom from sin was superior to the freedom of the city. During the long, medieval obsolescence of the civic, the claim for an active membership in the political community was superseded by the exigencies of just governance, and civic excellence was abbreviated to martial virtue.

Once citizenship was equated with human dignity, its extension to all classes, professions, both sexes, all races, creeds, and locations was only a matter of time. Universal franchise, the national service, and state education for all had to follow. Moreover, once all human beings were supposed to be able to accede to the high rank of a citizen, national solidarity within the newly egalitarian political community demanded the relief of the estate of Man, a dignified material existence for all, and the eradication of the remnants of personal servitude. The state, putatively representing everybody, was prevailed upon to grant not only a modicum of wealth for most people, but also a minimum of leisure, once the exclusive temporal fief of gentlemen only, in order to enable us all to play and enjoy the benefits of culture.

For the liberal, social-democratic, and other assorted progressive heirs of the Enlightenment, then, progress meant universal citizenship—that is, a virtual equality of political condition, a virtually equal say for all in the common affairs of any given community—together with a social condition and a model of rationality that could make it possible. For some, socialism seemed to be the straightforward continuation and enlargement of the Enlightenment project; for some, like Karl Marx, the completion of the project required a revolution (doing away with the appropriation of surplus value and an end to the social division of labor). But for all of them it appeared fairly obvious that the merger of the human and the political condition was, simply, moral necessity.

The savage nineteenth-century condemnations of bourgeois society—the common basis, for a time, of the culturally avant-garde and politically radical—stemmed from the conviction that the process, as it was, was fraudulent, and that individual liberty was not all it was cracked up to be, but not from the view, represented only by a few solitary figures, that the endeavor was worthless. It was not only Nietzsche and Dostoevsky who feared that increasing equality might transform everybody above and under the middle classes into bourgeois philistines. Progressive revolutionaries, too, wanted a New Man and a New Woman, bereft of the inner demons of repression and domination: a civic community that was at the same time *the* human community needed a new morality grounded in respect for the hitherto excluded.

This adventure ended in the debacle of 1914. Fascism offered the most determined response to the collapse of the Enlightenment, especially of democratic socialism and progressive social reform. Fascism, on the whole, was not conservative, even if it was counter-revolutionary: it did not re-establish hereditary aristocracy or the monarchy, despite some romantic-reactionary verbiage. But it was able to undo the key regulative (or liminal) notion of modern society, that of universal citizenship. By then, governments were thought to represent and protect everybody. National or state borders defined the difference between friend and foe; foreigners could be foes, fellow citizens could not. *Pace* Carl Schmitt, the legal theorist of fascism and the political theologian of the Third Reich, the sovereign could *not* simply decide by fiat who would be friend and who would be foe. But Schmitt was right on one fundamental point: the idea of universal citizenship contains an inherent contradiction in that the dominant institution of modern society, the nation-state, is both a universalistic and a parochial (since territorial) institution. Liberal nationalism, unlike ethnicism and fascism, is limited—if you wish, tempered—universalism. Fascism put an end to this shilly-shallying: the sovereign was judge of who does and does not belong to the civic community, and citizenship became a function of his (or its) trenchant decree.

THIS HOSTILITY TO UNIVERSAL CITIZENSHIP is, I submit, the main characteristic of fascism. And the rejection of even a tempered universalism is what we now see repeated under democratic circumstances (I do not even say under democratic disguise). Post-totalitarian fascism is thriving under the capacious carapace of global capitalism, and we should tell it like it is.

There is logic in the Nazi declaration that communists, Jews, homosexuals, and the mentally ill are non-citizens and, therefore, non-human. (The famous ideologist of the Iron Guard, the suave essayist E. M. Cioran, pointed out at the time that if some persons are non-human but aspire to humanity [i.e., Jews] the contradiction might be sublated and resolved by their violent death, preferably, according to the celebrated and still-fashionable aesthete, by their own hand.)

These categories of people, as the Nazis saw them, represented types crucial to the Enlightenment project of inclusion. Communists meant the rebellious "lower type," the masses brought in, leaderless and rudderless, by rootless universalism, and then rising up against the natural hierarchy; Jews, a community that survived the Christian middle ages without political power of its own, led by an essentially non-coercive authority, the people of the Book, by definition not a people of war; homosexuals, by their inability or unwillingness to procreate, bequeath, and continue, a living refutation of the alleged link between nature and history; the mentally ill, listening to voices unheard by the rest of us—in other words, people whose recognition needs a moral effort and is not immediately ("naturally") given, who can fit in only by enacting an equality of the unequal.

Everywhere, from Lithuania to California, immigrant and even autochthonous minorities have become the enemy.

The perilous differentiation between citizen and non-citizen is not, of course, a fascist invention. As Michael Mann points out in a pathbreaking study, the classical expression "We the People" did not include black slaves and "red Indians" (Native Americans), and the ethnic, regional, class, and denominational definitions of "the people" have led to genocide both "out there" (in settler colonies) and within nation states (see the Armenian massacre perpetrated by modernizing Turkish nationalists) under democratic, semi-democratic, or authoritarian (but not "totalitarian") governments. If sovereignty is vested in the people, the territorial or demographic definition of what and who the people are becomes decisive. Moreover, the withdrawal of legitimacy from state socialist (communist) and revolutionary nationalist ("Third World") regimes with their mock-Enlightenment definitions of nationhood left only racial, ethnic, and confessional (or denominational) bases for a legitimate claim or title for "state-formation" (as in Yugoslavia, Czechoslovakia, the ex-Soviet Union, Ethiopia-Eritrea, Sudan, etc.).

Everywhere, then, from Lithuania to California, immigrant and even autochthonous minorities have become the enemy and are expected to put up with the diminution and suspension of their civic and human rights. The propensity of the European Union to weaken the nation-state and strengthen regionalism (which, by extension, might prop up the power of the center at Brussels and Strasbourg) manages to ethnicize rivalry and territorial inequality (see Northern vs. Southern Italy, Catalonia vs. Andalusia, English South East vs. Scotland, Fleming vs. Walloon Belgium, Brittany vs. Normandy). Class conflict, too, is being ethnicized and racialized, between the established and secure working class and lower middle class of the metropolis and the new immigrant of the periphery, also construed as a problem of security and crime. Hungarian and Serbian ethnicists pretend that the nation is wherever persons of Hungarian or Serbian origin happen to live, regardless of their citizenship, with the corollary that citizens of their nation-state who are ethnically, racially, denominationally, or culturally "alien" do not really belong to the nation.

The growing de-politicization of the concept of a nation (the shift to a cultural definition) leads to the acceptance of discrimination as "natural." This is the discourse the right intones quite openly in the parliaments and street rallies in Eastern and Central Europe, in Asia, and, increasingly, in "the West." It cannot be denied that attacks against egalitarian welfare systems and affirmative action techniques everywhere have a dark racial undertone, accompanied by racist police brutality and vigilantism in many places. The link, once regarded as necessary and logical, between citizenship, equality, and territory may disappear in what the theorist of the Third Way, the formerly *Marxissant* sociologist Anthony Giddens, calls a society of responsible risk-takers.

The most profound attempt to analyze the phenomenon of political exclusion is Georges Bataille's "The Psychological Structure of Fascism," which draws on the author's distinction between homogeneity and heterogeneity. To simplify, homogeneous society is the society of work, exchange, usefulness, sexual repression, fairness, tranquility, procreation; what is heterogeneous

> includes everything resulting from *unproductive* expenditure (sacred things themselves form part of this whole). This consists of everything rejected by *homogeneous* society as waste or as superior transcendent values. Included are the waste products of the human body and certain analogous matter (trash, vermin, etc.); the parts of the body; persons, words, or acts having a suggestive erotic value; the various unconscious processes such as dreams and neuroses; the numerous later elements or social forms that *homogeneous* society is powerless to assimilate (mobs, the warrior, aristocratic and impoverished classes, different types of violent individuals or at least those who refuse the rule—madmen, leaders, poets, etc.); ... *violence, excess, delirium, madness* characterize heterogeneous

elements . . . compared to everyday life, *heterogeneous* existence can be represented as something *other*, as *incommensurate*, by charging these words with the *positive* value they have in *affective* experience.

Sovereign power, according to Bataille (and to Carl Schmitt), is quintessentially heterogeneous in its premodern sacral versions (kings ruling by Divine Right). This heterogeneity is hidden in capitalist democracy, where the sovereign is supposed to rule through an impersonal legal order that applies equally to all. Fascist dictatorship is in business to uncover or unmask it. This explains the link of fascist dictatorship to the impoverished, disorderly, *lumpen* mob. And this is exactly, I should add, what gets lost in post-fascism. The re-creation of sacral sovereignty by fascism is, however, a fake. It is homogeneity masquerading as heterogeneity. What is left in the homogeneous sphere in the middle is the pure bourgeois without the *citoyen*, Julien Sorel finally and definitely robbed of his Napoleon, Lucien Leuwen deprived of his Danton. Fascism, having put an end to the bourgeois realization of Enlightenment (i.e., to egalitarian capitalist democracy), transforms the social exclusion of the unproductive (from hermits and vatic poets to unemployable paupers and indomitable rebels) into their natural exclusion (i.e., extralegal arrest, hunger, and death).

Bataille's work comes out of the French objectivist sociological tradition, from Durkheim, Mauss, and Halbwachs through Kojève to Paul Veyne, wherein political repression and exclusion are not interpreted in moralistic and psychological, but in anthropological terms—as a matter of establishing identity. Bataille's revolutionary critique of the exclusion of the "heterogeneous"—the "useless," people who are not "responsible risk-takers"—is based on an understanding of society, sexuality, and religion, a combination of Durkheim and Marx, if you wish, that might offer an alternative of our contemporary, on the whole Kantian, resistance to post-fascism. Our moralistic criticism, however justified, customarily precludes the comprehension of the lure of the phenomenon, and leads to a simplistic contempt for barbaric, benighted racists, rabble-rousers, and demagogues, and a rather undemocratic ignorance of peoples, fears, and desires.

An alternative line of argument, suggested by this tradition, begins by observing that the breakdown of egalitarian welfare states frequently means a shift in the focus of solidarity, fraternity, and pity. If there is no virtually equal citizenship, the realization of which should have been the aim of honest, liberal democrats and democratic socialists, the passion of generosity will remain dissatisfied. A feeling of fellowship toward kith and kin has always been one of the most potent motives for altruism. Altruism of this kind, when bereft of a civic, egalitarian focus, will find intuitive criteria offered by the dominant discourse to establish what and whom it will desire to serve. If civic politics cannot do it, racial feeling or feelings of cultural proximity certainly will. Identity is usually outlined by affection and received threats. He who will define those successfully wins. Nobody is better at describing this *identity panic* than Bataille.

THE HALF-MAD PORNOGRAPHER and ultraleftist extremist, as Bataille is still regarded *in petto*, cannot be well received by self-respecting social theorists, I believe, but curiously his theory is borne out by the acknowledged standard work on the Nazi regime, written by the greatest legal hawk of the German trade union movement, happily rediscovered today as the first-rate mind that he was. In contradistinction to fanciful theories of totalitarianism, the great Ernst Fraenkel, summing up his painstaking survey of Nazi legislation and jurisprudence, writes in 1937–39 that

> in present day Germany, many people find the arbitrary rule of the Third Reich unbearable. These same people acknowledge, however, that the idea of "community," as there understood, is something truly great. Those who take up this ambivalent attitude toward National-Socialism suffer from two principal misconceptions:
>
> 1. The present German ideology of *Gemeinschaft* (community) is nothing but a mask hiding the still existing capitalistic structure of society.
>
> 2. The ideological mask (the community) equally hides the Prerogative State [Fraenkel distinguishes the "normal," so-called Normative State providing chiefly for civil law and the quasi-totalitarian Party state subordinated to the *Führerprinzip*] operating by arbitrary measures.

The replacement of the *Rechtsstaat* (Legal State) by the Dual State is but a symptom. The root of evil lies at the exact point where the uncritical opponents of National-Socialism discover grounds for admiration, namely in the community ideology and in the militant capitalism which this very notion of the *Gemeinschaft* is supposed to hide. It is indeed for the maintenance of capitalism in Germany that the authoritarian Dual State is necessary.

The Autonomy of the Normative State ("homogeneous society") was maintained in Nazi Germany in a limited area, mostly where the protection of private property was concerned (property of so-called Aryans, of course); the Prerogative State held sway in more narrowly political matters, the privileges of the Party, the military and the para-military, culture, ideology, and propaganda. The "dual state" was a consequence of the Schmittian decision of the new sovereign as to what was law, and what was not. But there was no rule by decree in the sphere reserved to capitalism proper, the economy. It is not true, therefore, that the *whole* system of Nazi or fascist governance was *wholly* arbitrary. The macabre meeting of the Normative and the Prerogative is illustrated by the fact that the German Imperial Railways billed the SS for the horrible transports to Auschwitz at special holiday discount rates, customary for package tours. But they billed them!

Sans Führer, *sans* one-party rule, *sans* SA or SS, post-fascism reverses the Enlightenment tendency to assimilate citizenship to the human condition.

People within the jurisdiction of the Normative State (Bataille's homogeneous society) enjoyed the usual protection of law, however harsh it tended to be. Special rules, however, applied to those in the purview of the Prerogative State (heterogeneous society)—both the Nazi Party leaders, officials, and militant activists, above the law, and the persecuted minorities, under or outside it. Before fascism, friend and citizen, foe and alien, were coincidental notions; no government thought systematically to declare war on the inhabitants of the land, who were members (even if unequal members) of the nation: civil war was equated with the absence of legally constituted, effective government. Civil war from the top, launched in peacetime, or at least under definitely non-revolutionary circumstances, turns sovereignty against the suzerain of the subject. The main weapon in this methodical civil war, where the state as such is one of the warring parties, is the continuous redefinition of citizenship by the Prerogative state.

And since, thanks to Enlightenment, citizenship (membership in the political community), nationality, and humanity had been synthetically merged, being expelled from citizenship meant, quite literally, exclusion from humanity. Hence civic death was necessarily followed by natural death, that is, violent death, or death *tout court*. Fascist or Nazi genocide was not preceded by legal condemnation (not even in the stunted and fraudulent shape of the so-called administrative verdicts of Cheka "tribunals"): it was the "naturalization" of a moral judgment that deemed some types of human condition inferior. And since there was no protection outside citizenship, lack of citizenship had become the cause of the cessation of the necessary precondition of the human condition—life.

CUTTING THE CIVIC AND HUMAN COMMUNITY in two: this is fascism.

This is why the expression, albeit bewildering, must be revived, because the fundamental conceptual technique of civic, hence human, scission has been revived, this time not by a deliberate counter-revolutionary movement, but by certain developments that were, probably, not willed by anyone and that are crying out for a name. The name is post-fascism.

The phenomenon itself came into being at a confluence of various political processes. Let me list them.

Decline of Critical Culture

After the 1989 collapse of the Soviet bloc, contemporary society underwent fundamental change. Bourgeois society, liberal democracy, democratic capitalism—name it what you will—has always been a controversial affair; unlike previous regimes, it developed an adversary culture, and was permanently confronted by strong competitors on the right (the alliance of the throne and the altar) and the left (revolutionary socialism). Both have become obsolete, and this has created a serious crisis within the culture of late modernism. The mere idea of radical change (utopia and critique) has been dropped from the rhetorical vocabulary, and the political horizon is now filled by what is there, by what is given, which is capitalism. In the prevalent social imagination, the whole human cosmos is a "homogeneous society"—a society of useful, wealth-producing, procreating, stable, irreligious, but at the same time jouissant, free individuals. Citizenship is increasingly defined, apolitically, in terms of interests that are not contrasted with the common good, but united within it through understanding, interpretation, communication, and voluntary accord based on shared presumptions.

In this picture, obligation and coercion, the *differentia specifica* of politics (and in permanent need of moral justification), are conspicuously absent. "Civil society"—a nebula of voluntary groupings where coercion and domination, by necessity, do not play any important role—is said to have cannibalized politics and the state. A dangerous result of this conception might be that the continued underpinning of law by coercion and domination, while criticized *in toto*, is not watched carefully enough—since, if it cannot be justified at all, no justification, thus no moral control, will be sought. The myth, according to which the core of late-modern capitalism is "civil society," blurs the conceptual boundaries of citizenship, which is seen more and more as a matter of policy, not politics.

Before 1989, you could take it for granted that the political culture of liberal-democratic-constitutional capitalism was a critical culture, more often than not in conflict with the system that, sometimes with bad grace and reluctantly, sustained it. Apologetic culture was for ancient empires and anti-liberal dictatorships. Highbrow despair is now rampant. But without a sometimes only implicit utopia as a prop, despair does not seem to work. What is the point of theoretical anti-capitalism, if political anti-capitalism cannot be taken seriously?

Also, there is an unexpected consequence of this absence of a critical culture tied to an oppositional politics. As one of the greatest and most level-headed masters of twentieth-century political sociology, Seymour Martin Lipset, has noted, fascism is the *extremism of the center*. Fascism had very little to do with *passéiste* feudal, aristocratic, monarchist ideas, was on the whole anti-clerical, opposed communism and socialist revolution, and—like the liberals whose electorate it had inherited—hated big business, trade unions, and the social welfare state. Lipset had classically shown that extremisms of the left and right were by no means exclusive: some petty bourgeois attitudes suspecting big business and big government could be, and were, prolonged into an extremism that proved lethal. Right-wing and center extremisms were combined in Hungarian, Austrian, Croatian, Slovak para-fascism (I have borrowed this term from Roger Griffin) of a pseudo-Christian, clericalist, royalist coloring, but extremism of the center does and did exist, proved by Lipset also through continuities in electoral geography.

Today there is nothing of any importance on the political horizon but the bourgeois center, therefore its extremism is the most likely to reappear. (Jörg Haider and his Freedom Party are the best example of this. Parts of his discourse are libertarian/neoliberal, his ideal is the propertied little man, he strongly favors a shareholding and home-owning petty bourgeois "democracy," and he is quite free of romantic-reactionary nationalism as distinct from parochial selfishness and racism.) What is now considered "right-wing" in the United States would have been considered insurrectionary and suppressed by armed force in any traditional regime of the right as individualistic, decentralizing, and opposed to the monopoly of coercive power by the government, the foundation of each and every conservative creed. Conservatives are *le parti de l'ordre* and loathe militias and plebian cults.

Decaying States

The end of colonial empires in the 1960s and the end of Stalinist ("state socialist," "state capitalist," "bureaucratic collectivist") systems in the 1990s has triggered a process never encountered since the Mongolian invasions in the thirteenth century: a comprehensive and apparently irreversible collapse of established statehood as such. While the *bien-pensant* Western press daily bemoans perceived threats of dictatorship in faraway places, it usually ignores the reality behind the tough talk of powerless leaders, namely that nobody is prepared to obey them. The old, creaking, and unpopular nation-state—the only institution to date that had been able to grant civil rights, a modicum of social assistance, and some protection from the exactions of privateer gangs and rapacious, irresponsible business elites—ceased to exist or never even emerged in the majority of the poorest areas of the world. In most parts of sub-Saharan Africa and of the former Soviet Union not only the refugees, but the whole population could be considered stateless. The way back, after decades of demented industrialization (see the horrific story of the hydroelectric plants everywhere in the Third World and the former Eastern bloc), to a subsistence economy and "natural" barter exchanges in the midst of environmental devastation, where banditry seems to have become the only efficient method of social organization, leads exactly nowhere. People in Africa and ex-Soviet Eurasia are dying not by a surfeit of the state, but by the absence of it.

The field was chosen by post-fascism, and liberals are mistakenly trying to fight it on its own favorite terrain: ethnicity.

Traditionally, liberation struggles of any sort have been directed against entrenched privilege. Equality came at the expense of ruling groups: secularism reduced the power of the Princes of the Church, social legislation dented the profits of the "moneyed interest," universal franchise abolished the traditional political class of landed aristocracy and the *noblesse de robe,* the triumph of commercial pop culture smashed the ideological prerogatives of the progressive intelligentsia, horizontal mobility and suburban sprawl ended the rule of party politics on the local level, contraception and consumerist hedonism dissolved patriarchal rule in the family—something lost, something gained. Every step toward greater freedom curtailed somebody's privileges (quite apart from the pain of change). It was conceivable to imagine the liberation of outlawed and downtrodden lower classes through economic, political, and moral crusades: there was, crudely speaking, somebody to take ill-gotten gains from. And those gains could be redistributed to more meritorious sections of the population, offering in exchange greater social concord, political tranquility, and safety to unpopular, privileged elites, thereby reducing class animosity. But let us not forget though that the social-democratic bargain has been struck as a result of centuries of conflict and painful renunciations by the traditional ruling strata. Such a liberation struggle, violent or peaceful, is not possible for the new wretched of the earth.

Nobody exploits them. There is no extra profit and surplus value to be appropriated. There is no social power to be monopolized. There is no culture to be dominated. The poor people of the new stateless societies—from the "homogeneous" viewpoint—are totally superfluous. They are not exploited, but neglected. There is no overtaxation, since there are no revenues. Privileges cannot be redistributed toward a greater equality since there are no privileges, except the temporary ones to be had, occasionally, at gunpoint.

Famished populations have no way out from their barely human condition but to leave. The so-called center, far from exploiting this periphery of the periphery, is merely trying to keep out the foreign and usually colored destitutes (the phenomenon is euphemistically called "demographic pressure") and set up awesome barriers at the frontiers of rich countries, while our international financial bureaucracy counsels further deregulation, liberalization, less state, and less government to nations that do not have any, and are perishing in consequence. "Humanitarian wars" are fought in order to prevent masses of refugees from flowing in and cluttering up the Western welfare systems that are in decomposition anyway.

Citizenship in a functional nation-state is the one safe meal ticket in the contemporary world. But such citizenship is now a privilege of the very few. The Enlightenment assimilation of citizenship to the necessary and "natural" political condition of all human beings has been reversed. Citizenship was once upon a time a privilege within nations. It is now a privilege to *most* persons in *some* nations. Citizenship is today the very exceptional privilege of the inhabitants of flourishing capitalist nation-states, while the majority of the world's population cannot even begin to aspire to the civic condition, and has also lost the relative security of pre-state (tribe, kinship) protection.

The scission of citizenship and sub-political humanity is now complete, the work of Enlightenment irretrievably lost. Post-fascism does not need to put noncitizens into freight trains to take them into death; instead, it need only prevent the new noncitizens from boarding any trains that might take them into the happy world of overflowing rubbish bins that could feed them. Post-fascist movements everywhere, but especially in Europe, are anti-immigration movements, grounded in the "homogeneous" worldview of productive usefulness. They are not simply protecting racial and class privileges within the nation-state (although they are doing that, too) but protecting universal citizenship within the rich nation-state against the virtual-universal citizenship of all human beings, regardless of geography, language, race, denomination, and habits. The current notion of "human rights" might defend people from the lawlessness of tyrants, but it is no defense against the lawlessness of no rule.

Varieties of Post-Fascism

It is frequently forgotten that contemporary global capitalism is a second edition. In the pre-1914 capitalism of no currency controls (the gold standard, etc.) and free trade, a world without visas and work permits, when companies were supplying military stuff to the armies of the enemy in wartime without as much as a squeak from governments or the press, the free circulation of capital and labor was more or less assured (it was, perhaps, a less equal, but a freer world). In comparison, the thing called "globalization" is a rather modest undertaking, a gradual and timorous destruction of *étatiste* and *dirigiste* welfarist nation-states built on the egalitarian bargain of old-style social democracy whose constituency (construed as the backbone of modern nations), the rust-belt working class, is disintegrating. Globalization has liberated capital flows. Speculative capital goes wherever investments appear as "rational," usually places where wages are low and where there are no militant trade unions or ecological movements. But unlike in the nineteenth century, labor is not granted the same freedoms. *Spiritus flat ubi vult*: capital flies wherever it wants, but the free circulation of labor is impeded by ever more rigid national regulations. The flow is all one-way; capital can improve its position, but labor—especially low-quality, low-intensity labor in the poor countries of the periphery—cannot. Deregulation for capital, stringent regulation for labor.

If the workforce is stuck at the periphery, it will have to put up with sweatshops. Attempts to fight for higher salaries and better working conditions are met *not* with violence, strikebreakers, or military coups, but by quiet capital flight and disapproval from international finance and its international or national bureaucracies, which will have the ability to decide who is deserving of aid or debt relief. To quote Albert O. Hirschman, *voice* (that is, protest) is impossible, nay, pointless. Only *exit*, exodus, remains, and it is the job of post-fascism to prevent that.

We are faced with a new kind of extremism of the center. Political participation of the have-nots is out of the question, without any need for the restriction of franchise.

Under these conditions, it is only logical that the New New Left has re-appropriated the language of human rights instead of class struggle. If you glance at *Die Tageszeitung*, *Il Manifesto*, *Rouge*, or *Socialist Worker* you will see that they are mostly talking about asylum-seekers, immigrants (legal or illegal, *les sans-papiers*) squatters, the homeless, Gypsies, and the like. It is a tactic forced upon them by the disintegration of universal citizenship, by unimpeded global capital flows, by the impact of new technologies on workers and consumers, and by the slow death of the global sub-proletariat. Also, they have to face the revival of class politics in a new guise by the proponents of "the third way" à la Tony Blair. The neo-neoliberal state has rescinded its obligations to "heterogeneous," non-productive populations and groups. Neo-Victorian, pedagogic ideas of "workfare," which declare unemployment implicitly sinful, the equation of welfare claimants with "enemies of the people," the replacement of social assistance with tax credits whereby people beneath the category of taxpayers are not deemed worthy of aid, income support made conditional on family and housing practices believed proper by "competent authorities," the increasing racialization, ethnicization, and sexualization of the underclass, the replacement of social solidarity with ethnic or racial solidarity, the overt acknowledgment of second-class citizenship, the tacit recognition of the role of police as a racial defense force, the replacement of the idea of emancipation with the idea of privileges (like the membership in the European Union, the OECD, or the WTO) arbitrarily dispensed to the deserving poor, and the transformation of rational arguments against EU enlargement into racist/ethnicist rabble-rousing—all this is part of the post-fascist strategy of the scission of the civic-cum-human community, of a renewed granting or denial of citizenship along race, class, denominational, cultural, ethnic lines.

The re-duplication of the underclass—a global underclass abroad and the "heterogeneous," wild ne'er-do-wells at home, with the interests of one set of underclass ("domestic") presented as inimical to the other ("foreign")—gives post-fascism its missing populist dimension. There is no harsher enemy of the immigrant—"guest worker" or asylum-seeker—than the obsolescent *lumpenproletariat* publicly represented by the hard-core, right-wing extremist soccer hooligan. "Lager louts" may not know that *lager* does not only mean a kind of cheap continental beer, but also a concentration camp. But the unconscious pun is, if not symbolic, metaphorical.

WE ARE, THEN, FACED with a new kind of extremism of the center. This new extremism, which I call post-fascism, does not threaten, unlike its predecessor, liberal and democratic rule within the core constituency of "homogeneous society." Within the community cut in two, freedom, security, prosperity are on the whole undisturbed, at least within the productive and procreative majority that in some rich countries encompasses nearly all white citizens. "Heterogeneous," usually racially alien, minorities are not persecuted, only neglected and marginalized, forced to live a life wholly foreign to the way of life of the majority (which, of course, can sometimes be qualitatively better than the flat workaholism, consumerism, and health obsessions of the majority). Drugs, once supposed to widen and raise consciousness, are now uneasily pacifying the enforced idleness of those society is unwilling to help and to recognize as fellow humans. The "Dionysiac" subculture of the sub-proletariat further exaggerates the bifurcation of society. Political participation of the have-nots is out of the question, without any need for the restriction of franchise. Apart from the incipient and feeble ("new new") left-wing radicalism, as isolated as anarcho-syndicalism was in the second half of the nineteenth century, nobody seeks to represent them. The conceptual tools once offered by democratic and libertarian socialism are missing; and libertarians are nowadays militant bourgeois extremists of the center, ultracapitalist cyberpunks hostile to any idea of solidarity beyond the *fluxus* of the global marketplace.

Post-fascism does not need stormtroopers and dictators. It is perfectly compatible with an anti-Enlightenment liberal democracy that rehabilitates citizenship as a grant from the sovereign instead of a universal human right. I confess I am giving it a rude name here to attract attention to its glaring injustice. Post-fascism is historically continuous with its horrific predecessor only in patches. Certainly, Central and East European antisemitism has not changed much, but it is hardly central. Since post-fascism is only rarely a movement, rather simply a state of affairs, managed as often as not by so-called center-left governments, it is hard to identify intuitively. Post-fascists do not speak usually of total obedience and racial purity, but of the information superhighway.

Everybody knows the instinctive fury people experience when faced with a closed door. Now tens of millions of hungry human beings are rattling the doorknob. The rich countries are thinking up more sophisticated padlocks, while their anger at the invaders outside is growing, too. Some of the anger leads to the revival of the Nazi and fascist *Gedankengut* ("treasure-trove of ideas"), and this will trigger righteous revulsion. But post-fascism is not confined to the former Axis powers and their willing ex-clients, however revolting and horrifying this specific sub-variant may be. East European Gypsies (Roma and Sinti, to give their politically correct names) are persecuted both by the constabulary and by the populace, and are trying to flee to the "free West." The Western reaction is to introduce visa restrictions against the countries in question in order to prevent massive refugee influx, and solemn summons to East European countries to respect human rights. Domestic racism is supplanted by global liberalism, both grounded on a political power that is rapidly becoming racialized.

Multiculturalist responses are desperate avowals of impotence: an acceptance of the ethnicization of the civic sphere, but with a humanistic and benevolent twist. These avowals are concessions of defeat, attempts to humanize the inhuman. The field had been chosen by post-fascism, and liberals are trying to fight it on its own favorite terrain, ethnicity. This is an enormously disadvantageous position. Without new ways of addressing the problem of global capitalism, the battle will surely be lost.

But the new Dual State is alive and well. A Normative State for the core populations of the capitalist center, and a Prerogative State of arbitrary decrees concerning non-citizens for the rest. Unlike in classical, totalitarian fascism, the Prerogative State is only dimly visible for the subjects of the Normative State: the essential human and civic community with those kept out and kept down is morally invisible. The radical critique pretending that liberty within the Normative State is an illusion is erroneous, though understandable. The denial of citizenship based not on exploitation, oppression, and straightforward discrimination among the denizens of "homogeneous society," but on mere exclusion and distance, is difficult to grasp, because the mental habits of liberation struggle for a more just redistribution of goods and power are not applicable. The problem is not that the Normative State is becoming more authoritarian. The problem is that it belongs only to a few. **BR**

Liverpool's Albert Dock, 1982. Image: Getty Images

LOST LIVERPOOL
Emily Baughan

Liverpool and the Unmaking of Britain
Sam Wetherell
Apollo, £25.00 (cloth)

IN 1945 a ship lay in wait on the River Mersey by Liverpool, then Britain's foremost imperial port. Stripped of its cargo and packed with bunk beds, the ship contained a hundred dazed Chinese dock-workers, who had been hauled from their beds at night and rounded up in police cars to be deported back to Shanghai, their wives and children never to be told what became of them. The seamen had made their way to

Liverpool decades ago, on lumbering, lonely cargo ships. During the war years, they had crewed vital shipments of food and weaponry, even as German bombs razed the docks that received their vessels. But for those ordering the deportations, their contributions mattered little.

The decision was the product of Britain's new welfare state—a decidedly utilitarian, not utopian, project with an infrastructure forged in war (think conscription, nationalization, rationing) and a singular, at times ruthless goal: full employment and economic modernization for the collective it served. Any population outside of that collective, imagined as the white national community, would be welcomed only so long as it was useful. Seen as obstructing progress, the Chinese dock-workers—who might have themselves unknowingly displaced returning British servicemen from their jobs—were cast aside.

What happens when a whole city gets cast aside? Postwar Liverpool, whose maritime industries declined as imperial trade waned in the era of decolonization, would soon find out. Once a gateway to the Atlantic, the port city's westerly position now divided it from growing trade with Europe. By the early 1980s, when the combined effects of stagflation and neoliberal economics were reconfiguring Britain's other northern industrial cities, seven in every eight of Liverpool's dock jobs had already been lost. Britain's welfare state was a workers' state, designed to fit the greatest possible number of the population for productive labor and have their needs met, in the main, by fairly waged employment. Now that work for all was a past horizon, that welfare state could not save Liverpool. As the "productive regimes that had summoned them" ceased to exist, writes Sam Wetherell, the people of Liverpool, like the Chinese seamen before them, became extraneous.

However, rather than a simple story of being "left behind," the fate of Liverpool and its people can tell us something about the future. The major intervention made by Wetherell's *Liverpool and the Unmaking of Britain*, a pacy and compassionate ode to Merseyside, is to flip our chronology: Liverpool is not a relic, the book argues, but a prophecy. In the twenty-first century, the processes that rendered Liverpool obsolete in the twentieth—rising prices, falling wages, chronic labor insecurity, homelessness, and health care failure—have become endemic. As more and more are abandoned by the economy and the state, the decline that befell Liverpool threatens to become our collective destiny.

HOW DID IT FEEL to be at the vanguard of Britain's obsolescence? Standing in the Liverpool Airport on a warm July day in 1964, one might barely have noticed. The Beatles were making their fêted return to their home city, suit-clad and stepping off a shimmering jet, about to be engulfed by fawning, fainting crowds. They would exit the airport, located in the new suburb of Speke. Here, cool water from Capel Celyn, a small Welsh village submerged to create a reservoir's worth of fresh water for the just-built council estates, flowed from novel indoor taps. From Speke, they would move toward a city center poised on the brink of regeneration, down newly paved roads fit for an era of mass motoring in a city known, briefly, as "Britain's Detroit"—a fitting moniker for a city that had celebrated the opening of a Ford factory in the suburb of Halewood just a year earlier. The Beatles, boys from Merseyside suburbs importing a version of American swing, encountered a city embracing industrial regeneration at a moment when it seemed to be working.

The forces that rendered Liverpool obsolete in the twentieth century have become endemic in the twenty-first.

During the 1960s, the manufacture of cars created 30,000 new jobs in Liverpool, almost half of them at the Halewood Ford factory. Ford bosses were wary about employing former dockworkers, who tended to be highly unionized and used to a level of autonomy afforded by seasonal shift patterns, which placed their labor in high demand. To acculture them to the monotonous rhythms of the factory, with its half-kilometer-long production line, all but the most conservative unions were barred from official negotiations. This mattered little to workers, who simply imported more organic forms of collective action directly from the docks. Wildcat strikes, absenteeism, and a dockers' practice known as "the welt"—where half the gang would work while the other rested—were used to push back against poor conditions. One group of recently hired workers, yearning for the autonomy of dock work as they kept up with the rapid tempo of the production line, put explosive powder under the peel of an orange that their foreman planned to eat for lunch. However, while the white working class had been temporarily rescued from obsolescence, others had been cast aside: by refusing to hire former seafarers, Ford had introduced a color bar by stealth. With the loss of maritime industry, it was Black men who struggled the most to find new, factory-based employment.

The problem of Liverpool's surplus population had always been framed in racial terms. In 1934, eugenicist sociologist David Caradog Jones had warned that there were exactly 74,010 too many people living on the Merseyside and that, because of their idleness and the ongoing mixing between the white working class and foreign seafarers, the "quality of the people" of Liverpool would decline. Long before the deportation of Chinese sailors at the end of the World War II, Liverpool was being made whiter. The waterfront area of Sailortown, a strip of migrant dormitories hosting sailors from across the empire, had been eradicated through rounds of slum clearance and, eventually, German bombs. Liverpool's Black population (mostly descendants of West African sailors) were pushed inland and out of sight to Toxteth, a neighborhood in Liverpool's inner city. As white workers were given new work and new homes, discriminatory hiring practices locked minorities out of jobs while racist housing policies kept Black families away from the suburbs. The few who slipped through often returned to Toxteth after facing relentless (and unimaginative) hostility: bricks through windows; dog excrement through letter boxes. Discriminatory police violence, stop-and-search laws, and endemic racism meted out by an almost entirely white police force intensified the containment of Liverpool's Black population in Toxteth's crumbling, subdivided former Victorian mansions.

They would not silently endure their treatment forever. 1981 saw the Toxteth Uprising (Wetherell rejects the term "riot" as implicitly delegitimizing), one of a series of violent clashes between the police and minority communities in Liverpool, London, Bristol, and Manchester. During the febrile nights of July, police fired tear gas into crowds, a violent tactic that had only previously been used in overtly imperial contexts (Burma, Malaya, Belfast). Targets of the tear gas included a three-year-old girl, cowering behind her parents in the back seat of a car. For Toxteth's minorities, the long nights of fighting were a rejection not only of relentless police violence, but the wider structures of governance that had pushed them into an overpoliced, under-resourced area of the city to begin with. For the police, though, they were simply outside the national community: not only surplus, but disposable.

Liverpool's white community would not have defined themselves as such. In the suburbs, the factories, and the city center (where less than 1 percent of shop workers were Black), whiteness was ubiquitous. Unlike comparable deindustrializing cities in the United States, (we might think of St. Louis, which has had a similar, book-length treatment by historian Walter Johnson), Liverpool had no history of planned segregation and thus no overt white separatist movements. Nonetheless, when threatened, the white community closed ranks. In one of Britain's most left-wing cities (with a City Council led by Trotskyites for much of the 1980s), a petition circulated by the Young Conservatives in support of police conduct in Toxteth was signed by over 5000 people. Police Chief Kenneth Oxford was never called to account for catalyzing (and then violently quelling) the uprising.

But the sympathies of Liverpool's white citizens lay in the wrong place. Obsolescence was coming for them, too. A month after the riots, Chancellor of the Exchequer Geoffrey Howe wrote a memo to Prime Minister Margaret Thatcher, suggesting that "managed decline" might be the best strategy for Liverpool. The economic shocks of the 1970s had obliterated the optimism of the 1960s. Car factories had closed, and the inhabitants of the once-gleaming suburbs were now unemployed too. By the mid-1980s, just 7 percent of sixteen-year-old high-school leavers in Knowsley were finding employment. Wrote one resident, "If they send the career officer to schools, then they should send the dole officer, too."

Liverpool's white working class could have seen their own fate prophesied in Toxteth. In 1989, across the Pennines in Sheffield, police responded to chaos at the Hillsborough football stadium, created by their own incompetence, with murderous inaction. Having forced fans to enter the stadium through a few congested turnstiles, the police then failed to allow a heaving crowd out of a closed pen. Ninety-four people were crushed to death in the first minutes of the FA Cup Semi-Final (three more would die of their injuries in the years to come). Fans of Nottingham Forest, the opposing team, looked on in horror; police with contempt. For Wetherell, this defining moment in Liverpool's history was a "catastrophe made possible by the cheapening of the lives of people deemed to be surplus in a city that was derelict and abandoned." The tragedy not only happened *to* Liverpool but was *about* it. By the 1980s, the tracksuited "scouser" had become an emblem not of a lost Britain, but of its annoying afterlife. A surplus, threatening masculinity, prone to alcoholism, casual violence, and identification with region over nation, incarnated a new tabloid trope: the football hooligan.

Writing this a mere mile from Hillsborough, I wondered if Sheffield's own obsolescence was also partly to blame for the tragedy that unfolded on a warm spring Saturday afternoon. Sheffield, a steel city, had like Liverpool entered its own terminal decline ahead of the national curve. The rapid growth of sites of steel production in the newly industrializing world meant that British steel ceased to be profitable before British coal did. Sheffield's working class had been staring down their own obsolescence before Thatcher and Thatcherism, much like Liverpool's dockworkers had after the decline of imperial trade. The utopianism of Sheffield's iconic urban housing developments—most famous a Le Corbusier–style development named Park Hill—could not outlast the city's economic boom. Conditions declined and crime rose from the beginning of the 1970s, and the South Yorkshire Police devoted increasing resources to the problem of white, working-class male "youths."

By 1984, when the northernmost outskirts of the city were losing mining jobs as Thatcher's government tried to shed the financial burden of nationalized coal production, the most violent clash of Britain's two-year standoff between the state miners fighting for their profession and the South Yorkshire Police, the "Battle of Orgreave," erupted. Mounted officers charged their horses into an unarmed crowd, displaying a contempt for working-class life honed across a decade of economic decline in Sheffield. Just five years later, many of the same officers watched coolly as the bodies of the ninety-seven dead were laid out across the floor of an adjacent gym, even taking blood samples from the corpses of children in an attempt to establish that they had been drinking, that the dead had been culpable.

THE HISTORIOGRAPHY OF MODERN BRITAIN lacks its own Ruth Wilson Gilmore, whose *Golden Gulag* showed how in California, rises in policing and incarceration were a response to both labor surplus and the privatization of state security. Neoliberal economics, she shows, entailed not simply the shrinkage of the state but the expansion of its penal functions. In *Liverpool and the Unmaking of Britain*, increasingly violent policing, as it came for the Black community and then the white working class, figures merely as regrettable overreach on the part of the local and national government. Wetherell's analysis, while it gestures toward the ways working-class obsolescence conditioned policing (and incarceration), stops short of drawing the conclusion it points toward: that the violence was not simply born of an excess of contempt on the part of the police but was legitimated and even encouraged by a state that had designated particular populations as surplus.

Obsolescence enables not only chronic neglect, but active harm: this is the vital connective tissue between the clinical dispassion of neoliberal cuts in the last century and the intentional damage wrought by austerity in this one. Thatcherite economics were never disavowed in British politics, despite thirteen years of Labor rule beginning in 1997. What arrived in 2010 was a new austerity conservatism, committed to reducing national debt by cutting public services. Austerity was an international economic phenomenon, a response to the 2008 financial crisis that gave rise to regimes of similar scenes across Europe and the Americas.

In Britain, it had a particular class and cultural politics. It unevenly targeted the post-industrial working class by cutting revenues sent by central governments to local councils, which otherwise relied on the rates paid by local people. Because local council income matched local population wealth, wealth gaps between white-collar and blue-collar towns, between the North and South of England, became chasms. Liverpool, the third-poorest city council in the country, lost 35 percent of its local council budget between 2010 and 2023, and in the process racked up almost £600 million in debt. As inequality widened, a cultural campaign against the unemployed intensified, epitomized by *Benefits Street,* a sneering, fly-on-the-wall style reality series about the lives of unemployed council estate dwellers in Northern former industrial towns. The condition of labor surpluses—of obsolescence—was once again regarded as a moral failing. David Caradog Jones—who had written of idleness as inherently degrading as he travelled Liverpool's slums in the 1930s—found his acolytes in the twenty-first century tabloid press.

The very brief social-democratic window, during which unemployment was a collective problem demanding state solutions, had closed.

Every April 15, Liverpool "Remembers the Ninety-Seven" who lost their lives at Hillsborough. But even before the fateful semifinal match, social murder—that is, facilitating and hastening the death of particular groups through chronic neglect—was taking place on a scale both grander and more quotidian. In Britain, the life expectancy of working-class people decreased from the mid-1980s, most quickly in Liverpool. Chronic poverty, unemployment, and the neglect of housing stock created "deaths of despair" through suicide, substance abuse, and, more perniciously, unusually high rates of heart disease and cancer. Merseyside doctors began to talk about "shit life syndrome," a diagnosis that, in its mix of sympathy and pessimism, proved deadly: the large doses of opioids and benzodiazepines they prescribed paved the way for a heroin addiction crisis.

Merseyside doctors began to talk about "shit life syndrome," a diagnosis that proved deadly.

In Wetherell's formulation, Liverpool is "unmade," tossed aside by the state and capital when no longer useful. But there's a bit more to the story. It is not only that Liverpool's communities have been abandoned wholesale; they've been recycled and repurposed. After ceasing to be producers of private wealth, a working class left with the physical legacies of their labor become consumers of health care. Gabriel Winant has shown how in Pittsburgh, as factories closed, hospitals grew, adding more beds and more caretaking jobs to mend the broken bodies left behind. The same has happened in Liverpool. Though the National Health Service remains publicly funded, many of its functions are now outsourced to private companies. Health and social care—mostly, that is, care for the disabled and the elderly subcontracted to private providers—now accounts for 70 percent of local council spending. The bodies of the longshoreman and factory workers cast aside by deindustrialization now generate revenue for these private equity firms, many of which are headquartered in tax havens beyond Britain's shores. Liverpool, once a node through which wealth flowed into the United Kingdom, has become its exit point.

Wetherell is less interested in these dynamics, choosing instead to trace a more starkly visible history: how the workless working class became a product for consumption. In 1982, an editorial in the tabloid *Daily Mirror* had commented that—so fascinating was the speed of Liverpool's decline—its council should "put a fence around and charge for admission." Just over two decades later, in 2004, Liverpool became a UNESCO world heritage site (ironically, the designation was stripped in 2021 on the grounds that the waterfront's historical character had been compromised), and its fastest growing economic sector was, and remains, tourism. At the heart of the redeveloped Albert Dock, once the arrival point of brandy, cotton, silk, and tobacco, stands the Museum of Liverpool, a slanting low-rise concrete structure designed to mimic trading ships. Opened in 2011, the Museum memorializes a lost working-class way of life. Cobbled terraces made of fiberglass, black-and-white films displaying the Blitz spirit of the 1940s, exhibitions dedicated to an aseptic "resistance" against an unspecified foe—all conjure an authentic but unthreatening lost way of life which, alongside the legacy of The Beatles, attracts 60 million visitors each year.

Tourism brought revenue, retail, and service work to Britain's third-poorest city. It also brought white middle-class university graduates with cultural sector aspirations. Slightly north of the Museum of Liverpool, young professionals can visit an outdoor sauna or drink cocktails on the banks of the Mersey. Affluent urban life thrums beneath the shadow of Liverpool's iconic Liver Building, once one of the tallest buildings in Europe and an icon of the city's former maritime wealth. But, Wetherell writes, beyond a gleaming veneer of prosperity, there is no return to the past. The rising river will see the Albert Dock underwater within the lifetimes of Liverpool's youngest citizens. But even before environmental catastrophe arrives, he warns: obsolescence "might be coming for us all."

Hasn't it already arrived? Liverpool's white working class have been living with their own obsolescence since the 1970s; its Black community since the 1940s. Is the "us all" simply the middle classes—the white-collar cultural-sector and education professionals now facing the existential threat of zero-hours contracts, AI, and, in Britain, a "left" government with no plans to reverse the fifteen years of austerity that preceded it? Still, if a once-insulated middle class is the next to be rendered obsolete, what might they learn from those who went before? Can they outrun the complacency of Liverpool's white working class, who themselves failed to see their own futures prophesied in the degradation of their Black neighbors? Could they—could we—resist?

IF THERE IS A RESISTANCE, Wetherell argues, it lies in mutual care. From the 1980s, Liverpool might have had the highest incidence of "deaths of despair" in England, but it did not become an epicenter for the AIDS pandemic, as public-health officials had expected for a city with a heroin problem. This was because the people of Liverpool refused to neglect all the city's most precarious "surplus" citizens. Founding the first large-scale needle exchange in Britain, a quiet collective of activists ensured the safety of drug users and sex workers alike. Meanwhile, for the predominantly gay men already infected with the disease, the Merseyside AIDS Support Group refused to consign the dying to lonely, frightened deaths. They organized buddy systems, yoga classes, and a retreat on the west coast of Ireland, where daily swims with dolphins served as a kind of "natural therapist." These forms of care were a radical refusal of obsolescence. Even the addicted, even the dying, deserved to live.

Before we refuse our mutual obsolescence, we must accept it. There is a freedom in this. Locating our value in work or, when that fails, the state, was always precarious. Even in the imagined golden age after the war and before Thatcherism, welfare was only for the chosen. New houses, new jobs, new schools were unevenly distributed, and white workers were favored. When social democracy gave way to neoliberal economics, the white working class were abandoned first by their employers and then the state, too. People's value cannot lie in the value they produce; if our value is vested in anything but our shared humanity, it is ultimately unstable. Read hopefully, *Liverpool and the Unmaking of Britain* provides a deeply humanist, universalist prescription to collective obsolescence: if none of us matter, all of us do.

In Liverpool, this lesson has never been more urgent. Before a baby born on the Merseyside today has seen floodwaters lapping at the foundations of the Liverpool Museum, it will face more imminent threats.

One third of children in Liverpool live in poverty. A senior pediatrician at Liverpool's Alder Hey Children's Hospital estimated that between 2015 and 2017, 500 children in England died from preventable, poverty-related conditions. There is no memorial quilt unfurled for these infants in Liverpool's cathedrals as there was for the AIDS dead in 1992; no annual minute of silence for them as for the ninety-seven who died at Hillsborough. But all these deaths are produced by the same twin forces of contempt and neglect.

A new universalism might propel us forward, but only so far. For to spend any time in Liverpool is to see that remembering has a politics, too. As the Albert Dock disappears, like the Welsh village of Capel Celyn before it, Liverpool both reveals the future and uncovers a past where all was not as it seemed. Even in Britain's boom years, parts of the nation were already being unmade. Even as plans were being drawn to rebuild Liverpool from the rubble of German bombs, Chinese seamen were being deported silently by night. **BR**

WHO'S AFRAID OF PROTEST?

Alex Gourevitch

O VER THE LAST YEAR and a half, American universities have rapidly destroyed the right to protest on campus. At the request of administrators, heavily armed police raided unarmed, nonviolent protesters opposing Israel's war on Gaza. Encampments have been forcibly cleared, while extreme punishment has been used as a tool of intimidation. Some 3,100 students have been detained or arrested, and thousands more face severe university discipline—suspension, expulsion, and loss of degree.

More recently, the Trump administration has exacted even more suppression. First it suspended $400 million of federal funding to Columbia, conditioning its restoration on accession to a range of outrageous demands whose fulfillment, the administration alleges, is necessary to protect Jewish students and comply with Title VI of the 1964 Civil Rights Act. Sixty other universities were subsequently threatened with the same shakedown. Since then, Columbia protester Mahmoud Khalil was disappeared, despite his possession of a green card; he was only the first. In response, several universities have adopted extremely restrictive speech codes and protest rules, developed new disciplinary procedures and task forces, ousted faculty, decimated whole departments, and imposed draconian punishments. Only when faced with something approaching a hostile government takeover have universities like Harvard started to fight back.

Many factors, in addition to moral cowardice and ideological agreement, help to explain why universities capitulated. Across the country, their budgets have grown increasingly reliant on federal funding, especially to support scientific research. The structures of university governance empower boards and presidents over faculty, students, and staff, while trustees, with deep ties to business and politics, typically have little connection to research and teaching or to the institution at large. Endowments are widely seen as indicators of prestige, not to be spent down to defend institutional integrity but constantly expanded through the cultivation of megadonors. Meanwhile, a vast class of administrators has ballooned over the last half century, rendering donor relations ever more transactional and student life both more consumerist and more surveilled. To top it off, many elite universities have forsaken institutional neutrality for an increasingly vocal social justice liberalism over the last decade, both in the messaging of campus leadership and in administrative meddling in speech and student affairs.

All this has left universities vulnerable to Trump's attacks. Working in tandem with well-organized networks of "anti-antisemitism" advocacy groups, the administration is wielding antidiscrimination laws and "safetyist" rationales the right has spent years attacking to carry out the "counterrevolution blueprint" that Manhattan Institute senior fellow Christopher Rufo laid out in December, calling for purging universities and the federal government of "left-wing ideologies."

How should we fight back against this new McCarthyism? And to what end? As teachers and students learn just how little control they have over campus, it is clear that we need not just a general defense of academic freedom but also a more specific and absolutist defense of the right to protest. A democratic society generally, and colleges and universities in particular, must protect the right to engage in public, disruptive acts—including those that feature open expressions of hostility to political views—even at the cost of some people feeling discomfort or even intense unease. That was the prevailing attitude toward protest on campus for the past several decades, and it served all students, as well as the mission and vitality of the university, well.

Indeed, after the social movements of the 1960s pushed their way onto campus, universities rightly came to tolerate—even celebrate—protest as an ordinary part of university life, viewing it as a sign of the life and health of a community devoted to collective learning. As former Columbia president Lee Bollinger put it in 2008, "the '60s were significant in establishing freedom of expression," both on campus and off. It was a mistake, he concluded, to bring in the NYPD after students occupied a Columbia administration building in 1968. Even crackdowns at the time were not as severe as they have been in recent months. At the peak of anti-Vietnam protests in 1969, when millions rather than thousands of students were marching and occupying, only around 4,000 students were arrested—a vastly smaller percentage than today.

The Gaza protests represent more than the public airing of dissent. They test whether public space on campus can be said to exist at all.

If history is any guide, rescuing the rights now being rolled back will require a range of tactics, including vigorous protest itself. It will also require building broad and unwavering consensus about the speciousness of the rationales being offered for today's draconian crackdowns. Those have taken three principal forms. First, the Gaza protests were said to be disruptive to the ordinary life of the community. Second, because protests took place on private property—the property of the university—protesters who refused to disperse were said to be trespassing. Third and perhaps most perniciously, university community members stated that they felt the protests were threatening or harmful, which schools appear to have interpreted as sufficient evidence of a "hostile environment" for Jewish and Israeli students that may violate Title VI.

All of these are bad justifications. When they are interpreted and applied as they have been in recent months, there can be no right to protest at all. That is an outcome anyone committed to the mission and health of the university, not to mention democracy in general, must emphatically reject.

ON THE MATTER of disruptiveness, it is true that some Gaza protests sometimes interfered with ordinary foot traffic. But unlike, say, a labor picket, last year's gatherings and encampments did not actually try to prevent anyone from getting where they were trying to go. Students could still access their dorms and classes; faculty could still go to their classrooms and offices, and staff could still access their workplaces. In a few controversial cases, ordinary traffic through a commons was blocked, such that people had to maneuver around the encampments. That was genuinely inconvenient, but only that. The available reporting makes clear that in the vast majority of cases, everyone could find their way to where they needed to be. Where protesters erected obstacles, the evidence suggests they usually did so to defend and protect themselves.

Protests can also be noisy—inescapably, since any right to protest must accommodate fervent dissent. The noise can make it harder to study and teach. But this has been a routine feature of thousands of campus protests. Universities have rightly tolerated them in the past, especially when participants make the effort, as they generally did last year, to keep noise levels down in evenings. More basically, if making noise is itself punishable—and severely so—then there is effectively no right to protest. Recognizing such a right entails tolerance for some measure of disruptiveness, with only the most serious disruption serving as a legitimate basis for punishment—and then only modest punishment, which recognizes the conscientious nature of the protest act.

A question, then, is whether protesters crossed the line into serious disruption. Some did occupy administration buildings and in a few cases noisily interrupted classes or libraries. Yet the weight of punishment for these actions has been massively disproportionate and historically unprecedented. The aim of these punishments is not to reinforce discipline in light of rule-breaking but to persecute individuals *for protesting*. And in particular, for protesting the actions of Israel and universities' connection to Israel.

The second justification for cracking down—trespass—drew less public attention, but hundreds of protesters were arrested, and some were even criminally prosecuted, on this basis. Whether protesters violated university property rights when refusing to disperse depends on what we think the rules governing campus property should be. Historically, those rules have not proscribed encampments. Colleges have tolerated them when protesters agitated against war, racism, and South African apartheid; in support of free speech, women's rights, the Occupy movement, and living wages for university employees; and in hopes of creating new university departments.

Universities have also long permitted the extended use of campus commons for deeply offensive, in-your-face protest. For two days in October last year, for example, the University of South Carolina permitted the pro-life Genocide Awareness Project to post large signs reading "Genocide Photos Ahead" along with graphic images of aborted fetuses next to Nazi flags and images of lynched bodies and people murdered during the Rwandan genocide. "The purpose of [this protest] is to bring the truth of abortion to campuses . . . and to actually get conversation started," the president of the university's College Republicans said. Despite its highly controversial message and messaging, the Genocide Awareness Project has visited college campuses across the country for twenty-six years. Other examples include the posting of large, disturbing images of animal testing, and a highly inflammatory anti-affirmative action "bake sale" at Texas Tech in which a conservative student group sold cookies that were priced differently based on the race or ethnicity of the student.

To be clear, the question of whether protesters demonstrating against Israel's war in Gaza were trespassing does not turn on matters of legal ownership. No one doubts that, formally speaking, the campus commons are the private property of the university. The university's legal control over space is a foundation of academic freedom. The ability of academics to research and teach freely is predicated on universities' capacity to decide for themselves how campus facilities may be used—subject, of course, to generally applicable laws, including antidiscrimination laws.

But universities are not just places of research and teaching. They are also communities where people live: where they work, play, study, sleep, argue, fall in love, pray, compete, credentialize, and develop themselves. To sustain this kind of community, universities don't just enjoy formal rights of self-government; they normally have public spaces or commons, which are not like other pieces of university property. A yard, field, or plaza is not the same as a library or classroom. First Amendment jurisprudence protects access to such "public fora." Technically, this law applies only to public universities, but there is no good reason that administrators of private colleges should not apply the same standard. A commons is not ungoverned, but it is less governed—precisely so that members of the community may give voluntary expression to their relationship to the community, including congregating for the purpose of protesting the university's rules and actions and its relation to the wider world.

In this sense, the Gaza protests, like all protests, represent more than the public airing of the views of university community members. They simultaneously test whether public space on campus can be said to exist at all. Universities deeply betrayed their nonprofit, educational mission—the key feature that distinguishes them from private corporations—when they asserted a property right to shut these protests down. And no doubt, fork-tongued administrators will resume touting this very mission when the same politicians insisting on crackdowns set out to tax their endowments or revoke their tax-exempt status.

So much for the first two rationales. What about the third? The most high-profile defense of crackdowns—in some ways, the most insidious—has been that, while protest might generally be tolerated, these particular protests caused harm, threatened violence, or constituted harassment against Jewish or Israeli students.

It is certainly true that a university must protect students from harm and harassment if it is to sustain the social and intellectual life of the community. Nobody can enjoy academic freedom and free speech if they face credible threats of harm for what they say or who they are, nor if they are burdened by a genuinely hostile environment that directly excludes them from participating in campus life. The problem is not mainly with this standard itself but with the way it has been interpreted. The available evidence suggests that administrators made calls solely on the basis of self-reported feelings rather than on findings of credible, imminent threats or systematic denial of access. When some students or faculty said they felt threatened or harassed, that in itself counted as incontrovertible evidence of threat or harassment. When they said they felt harmed, that counted as harm.

According to the American Jewish Council, for example, about half of U.S. Jewish students who saw the demonstrations reported feeling "unsafe on campus." Hillel, meanwhile, found large numbers stating that "stronger responses and consequences" would make them feel safer. Parents and some Jewish or pro-Israel organizations insisted that the protests created an unsafe environment for Jewish and Israeli students. House Minority Leader Hakeem Jeffries echoed these concerns when he invoked the existence of a "hostile academic environment" to explain why universities were warranted in imposing severe disciplinary measures. The idea may not seem on its face implausible. After all, Jews are a minority with their own history of horrific and violent persecution. If our norms and laws are designed to protect historically marginalized groups, Jews' own history would appear to lend urgency and credibility to students' claims that something must be done to assuage their feelings of vulnerability.

That is precisely the kind of claim advanced by groups such as the Harvard Jewish Alumni Alliance, which issued a report condemning a "hostile environment" on campus that has been cited by private lawsuits. "Someone I know was studying in [xxx] library," the group quotes one student complaining. "He couldn't focus because he was sitting next to ~15 people in Keffiyehs who wanted to write an op-ed in support of that proctor who had been let go. My friend didn't want to stick around and study for the math exam." Another states, "It's scary to walk through the protest. I usually walk through the back doors [or the] side entrances at [the] science center." Still another says, "I have this flight or fight reaction when waking up in the morning and hearing the protestors chanting. I can't always tell what they're chanting, but I always feel that fear, feel triggered, and I [don't want to] walk through them to find out what they're saying."

These and similar statements provide ample evidence that students felt vulnerable or disturbed by protests. But it is a grave mistake—a threat to everyone's liberty and a betrayal of democracy—to infer on this basis that protests created an objectively hostile environment and therefore warranted being shut down. Reasoning of this kind is far too broad and repressive because it fails to distinguish between subjective feelings and objective circumstances. Notably, feelings of unease would never suffice to meet the legal standard of a "hostile environment." Proving that one has been threatened or harassed requires objective evidence, not just a subjective sense of fear. And the evidence must demonstrate systematic and severe mistreatment, not just isolated inconvenience or discomfort. The statements above do nothing of the sort. Yet in the case of the Gaza protests, litigation-wary, donor-beholden administrators took them as justification for extraordinary repression.

That is perhaps one reason not just the crackdowns but the ensuing punishments were exceptionally severe. The point, evidently, was to chill speech and send a message: any actions that caused Jewish or Israeli students to feel uncomfortable would not be tolerated. On the rare occasions when there were individualized threats or credible reports of assault, instead of just investigating and punishing the individuals responsible, administrators used the existence of such threats to suppress the whole mass of nonviolent protesters.

WHILE ADMINISTRATORS and university leadership are the ones setting policy on campus, the broader politics of this issue have made it difficult to build a strong and effective consensus about how to handle offensive speech, especially when it comes to the aggressive expressions so typical of protest. The justification from subjective feelings is not new, and its invocation in recent months is not surprising. On the contrary, recent crackdowns are the coercive endpoint of a way of thinking about harm and harassment that has been developing on and off campus for a long time, coming from the left as well as the right.

On the progressive side, arguments for speech codes and deplatforming have relied on the claim that feelings of being "triggered," "traumatized," or otherwise disrespected are sufficient evidence that a line has been crossed and administrative intervention is required. Across a wide range of issues, especially related to race and gender, liberal and left-wing students have tried to ban speakers, cancel events, or otherwise suppress speech on grounds that it makes them feel unsafe. Even critics of Israel have taken this tack. When the UC San Diego branch of Turning Point USA displayed a sign saying "Israel aims to protect / Terrorists aim to kill" next to the Israeli and Palestinian flags in 2022, pro-Palestinian students demanded the statement be taken down because it was harmful, dangerous, and reinforced bias.

For their part, conservatives unquestioningly defend police who say they feel unsafe and therefore need yet more physical protections and legal permission to kill. (Never mind that police are safer today than they have been in fifty years.) As for campus life, the pro-life right evidently believes it is fine to scream about genocide in campus protests showing pictures of dead babies—unless they are Palestinian babies. And they have eagerly embraced inflated fears about antisemitism as a cudgel against universities. After decrying "cancel culture" for a decade, Rufo argued in February, the right should now embrace it.

These debates are playing out in a particular context: a society that has become obsessed, in deeply destructive ways, with safety and security.

In this climate, university and public officials have accepted an increasingly expansive understanding of what counts as a hostile environment. Instead of stating a precise and objective standard that distinguishes action from speech, they have deemphasized the need to demonstrate objective risks of physical violence or threatening property destruction. Instead, the question authorities are asking is much simpler: whether statements or symbols might cause psychological pain or generate feelings of vulnerability among certain groups. They have gradually redefined the right to *be* safe as a right to *feel* safe. In some cases, colleges have explicitly rewritten their policies and disciplinary procedures to incorporate this redefinition. As law professor David Pozen observes, Columbia's 1968 Rules of University Conduct were written to institutionalize a liberal speech regime open to a wide range of protest-related expression. But the university wrote a new, overlapping Standards and Discipline policy in 2022 that "places greater emphasis on shielding vulnerable students from discriminatory harassment" and does so in part by using "broader definitions of harassing and discriminatory speech," Pozen explains. Columbia's anti-genocide protesters were punished under these rules.

To be sure, these are complex issues. The most reasonable defense of the hostile environment standard stems from a desire to protect the equal rights of historically marginalized groups. (Title VI specifically bars discrimination and exclusion based on "race, color, and national origin," and executive orders since then have expanded its purview to other forms of exclusion.) Are we really meant to think that African American students can feel safe or welcome on campus, or otherwise participate as equal members of the community, when white supremacists can gather on the quad and freely express their views? Aren't some symbols, like a noose or a burning cross, so potent that they constitute credible and actionable threats in themselves? And aren't certain speech acts so painful or offensive that they constitute a legally proscribed hostile environment, making it impossible to live and study on campus?

Courts have been reluctant to rule this way, but more to the point, we shouldn't want them to, because accepting these kinds of restrictions is incompatible with the right to protest. Whatever the proper domain of the hostile environment concept, it was never meant to (and shouldn't) extend to protest. It is not just that protests involve political expression. They are a particular *kind* of political expression: public expressions of hostility toward political views and often the people who hold them. If applied to speech in the context of protest, the hostile environment standard—or any norm that takes feelings of fear and insecurity as grounds for intervention—would make protest impossible.

In addition to conflating hurt with harm in order to justify repression, proponents of recent crackdowns have borrowed familiar progressive arguments for deferring to the oppressed about the definition of oppression. Objective assessment of harm, harassment, or intimidation is criticized on the grounds that "you do not tell Jews what antisemitism is," echoing widespread claims about deferring to people of color, for example, over the meaning of racism. As one Tablet author put it in a 2018 article about antisemitism, "Those who experience a specific oppression get to define it" because only they understand "the complex systems that keep historically marginalized groups down." And what gets defined here is not just the meaning of some speech but what counts as actionable harm or fear.

Recent events reveal the exhaustion of this kind of argument. Over time, invocations of the hostile environment standard have created a precedent for expanding the capacity of authorities to suppress speech and protest on an arbitrary basis: namely, whether those who express feelings of vulnerability or harm happen to be powerful and influential. Consider that Muslims and Arabs, especially Palestinians, have also reported feeling unsafe on campus. Two recent exhaustive studies at Harvard even found that while only 15 percent of Jewish students reported feeling physically unsafe, some 47 percent of Muslim students felt the same, and where 61 percent of Jewish students worried about expressing their views, a whopping 92 percent of Muslim students also worried.

Yet there have been no similar crackdowns on pro-Israel protesters or counter-demonstrators or whoever is causing those feelings, much less a mountain of messaging from university leaders meant to assuage their feelings of vulnerability. Instead, hewing to subjective feelings of threat has meant granting the most elite voices the right to define oppression in ways that suit their interests. Hence groups like the Anti-Defamation League and the International Holocaust Remembrance Association are granted wide latitude to define antisemitism, even as broad swaths of Jews in the United States and elsewhere strenuously disagree. Following a similar logic, many institutions adopted Ibram Kendi's questionable definition of racism in the aftermath of the 2020 protests over the killing of George Floyd, in spite of deep misgivings about Kendi's views from scholars and activists of color.

At least some advocates for social justice have recognized the exhaustion of this too-easy interpretation of the hostile environment standard for quite some time, though they have not always found allies among fellow opponents of oppression. As Henry Louis Gates put it during the culture wars of the 1990s, increased limits on speech, like speech codes, "can turn a garden-variety bigot into a First Amendment martyr." Gates's point is more than a strategic one. In the long-run practice of democratic societies, suppressing speech makes it seem like your own views and arguments are weak—so weak that you need the help of coercive authorities.

It is important to recognize that these debates over legal and political principles are playing out in a particular context: a society that has become obsessed, in deeply destructive ways, with safety and security. Over the past few decades, amid broader panics over crime pervading

U.S. culture, universities have responded to concerns about the vulnerability of students as such—often voiced by over-anxious parents footing tuition bills—with greater and greater mechanisms of surveillance and control. The result is that, no matter how safe campuses already are, anxieties about student safety never abate.

Look no further than the proliferation of electronic keycards controlling access to all buildings throughout campus, the ever-expanding size and power of campus police forces, and the widespread use of security cameras and armed security guards. In these and other ways, universities have fashioned themselves as safety-guaranteeing institutions, and the university community has come to internalize that guarantee. The paternalistic orientation of the garrison university makes protests appear all the more dangerous—much more like a targeted threat or intolerable environment—rather than something uncomfortable and unpleasant but which university members can respond to on their own, without the intervention of administrators, much less police.

The less we can tolerate each other's freedom, the more we become subject to the authorities to whom we end up appealing for protection.

This politics of fear goes hand in hand with a neoliberal culture awash in the therapeutic consumerism born of ever steeper competition for access to a minimally comfortable way of life. In a society that increasingly segregates us into homogeneous communities, where resources are privately hoarded and precious few public spaces remain, encountering sharp disagreement of the kind expressed in protest is especially likely to generate a subjective sense of unease and fright. It's in these conditions that the "desire to shrink groups down to spaces of easy agreement," in the words of Mariame Kaba and Kelly Hayes, flourishes most.

The point is not that claims about feeling unsafe must be cynical efforts to silence or censure. Nor is it to contend that the feelings aren't real or that people should not have the feelings they do. Rather, the point is that claiming to feel vulnerable and unsafe cannot, in itself, decide the question of whether protest (and other forms of speech, for that matter) crosses the line. There has to be some likely and imminent threat of harm, or direct and individualized harassment and intimidation. The very idea that it is dangerous to distinguish between felt harm and administratively or legally actionable injury is a symptom of how thoroughly gutted our moral and political imaginations have become. It also demonstrates how sharply we have inverted the relationship between vulnerability and freedom—making civil liberties, like speech, dependent on first reassuring others that they will not be made to feel insecure. We have a right to be in secure possession of our freedoms, but only so long as everyone else has those same freedoms— which means others are free to say and do things that are disconcerting, unnerving, or otherwise make us feel vulnerable.

We must be uncompromising on this principle, regardless of everything else we might disagree about: the mere fact that someone feels, or even that large numbers of people feel, intimidated, uneasy, or hurt by protest does not imply any protesters have crossed a line. Democracy is demanding. Encountering intense and passionate opposition to our views is inevitably discomfiting—how could it be otherwise, when our deeply held beliefs are challenged? Refusing to make large affordances for discomfort by distinguishing it from genuine threats is flatly incompatible with a right to protest.

THIS PRINCIPLE HAS IMPLICATIONS for the way universities should adjudicate claims of harm and hostility in the context of protests. At a minimum, policies that would result in the suppression of an individual's speech, or disciplinary action for an individual's behavior, should be required to document evidence that goes beyond the fact that people say they feel hurt, unwelcome, or unsafe. And even in cases where that standard is met, administrators must tailor discipline only to the specific individual rather than engage in collective punishment.

Furthermore, while universities do have a right and responsibility to preserve the ability to hold classes and go about their daily business, they should look to the way they handled protest-related disruptions in the past, when punishments for violating reasonable time, place, and manner restrictions or other campus rules were rightly modest and proportionate. That was the right way to fit together the right to protest with other important features of university life. Columbia, for example, had not expelled anyone for protest since 1968, despite numerous acts since then that were more disruptive, damaging, or harmful than anything done by the students it has recently disciplined. And even then, the expulsion of Mark Rudd, chair of the university's Students for a Democratic Society chapter at the time, was predicated on his activity being other than peaceful. Until last year, Columbia had not expelled anyone for *nonviolent* protest activity since 1936, when one Robert Burke was kicked out for protesting the university's association with Nazism.

Of course, as long as universities remain deeply undemocratic and donor-driven, we should not expect administrators to make such calls evenhandedly or without error. Under pressure from trustees and counsel offices, they are likely to continue to act in ways that, on the whole, serve powerful interests and bottom lines rather than the public good of the university. But that isn't the only source of misrule. University leaders are incorporating wider norms that emphasize official protection of the most vulnerable as a reason for the limiting of everyone's liberty—the irony, of course, being that this has only ended up strengthening the very authorities that now make everyone's freedom even less secure.

Moreover, the bulk of us who share in campus life have power too, and the principle has implications for us as well—in particular, for the informal norms we use to interpret when boundaries are crossed as we agitate to make universities more democratic and the world more just. Most basically, we must contend with the question of how to decide, in the context of everyday life, what is tolerable and what instead requires the intervention of administrators or other authorities. Tolerating doesn't mean agreeing with, supporting, or promoting the content of any given protest, nor does it mean letting protests and other speech we find despicable go uncontested or unprotested themselves. But it does mean not inviting, engaging in, and empowering administrative suppression. It also means accepting that degree of inconvenience and heightened sense of tension.

There is no question that this can be difficult and painful. As a Jewish professor who witnessed a number of protests in person and saw even more online, I experienced the full range of reactions. I was disturbed by a number of antisemitic statements, while also hearing things that others thought were antisemitic but I did not. I recoiled at horrific celebrations of violence against Israelis and felt the same about grotesque celebrations of violence against Palestinians. I also heard people saying things that I thought defended inexcusable violence against people in Gaza, but which the speakers did not think promoted violence at all. But none of what I heard, even about violence, amounted to threats of imminent and likely harm directed at specific individuals, including myself. No doubt, tolerating repulsive speech comes easier for some than for some others. Because we live in a very unequal society, people participate in the life of the university with very unequal resources and levels of support. But these circumstances won't be transformed through the restriction of protests, enabled by a too-expansive sense of what is intimidating or threatening. The recent crackdown on campus protests, in the very language of protecting the vulnerable, shows the failure of that approach.

My argument might sound like insensitive finger-wagging — "don't be so fragile; be more resilient, like me" — or at least too unsympathetic to the reasons people feel vulnerable in the face of public hostility. But my point is not to attack personal character. Rather, it is to emphasize what we stand to lose by accepting the terms of these intrusions on our liberty. We have to resist how our institutions, including universities, promote a democratically incoherent and politically incapacitating sense of fragility. The less we can tolerate each other's freedom, the more we become subject to the authorities to whom we end up appealing for protection, which in turn encourages us to feel increasingly vulnerable to each other.

A more permissive attitude toward protests might well create a campus culture that some find alienating. But on campuses that are supposed to be open to all members of society and that also include a significant international population, there is no better alternative than protecting *everyone's* right to protest. That is the only way, in fact, to guarantee that everyone is secure in the right way: not from feelings of fear, disgust, or alienation, but from authorities who would deny our freedom to raise our voices. Adopting this perspective means expecting of ourselves and of each other that we tolerate, or better yet counter-protest, when we can't stand what we see and hear. The main role of university leaders should be ensuring that protesters don't become violent toward each other—a role that administrators at UCLA, for example, failed at spectacularly even while also failing to defend the right to protest.

Everyone is made more vulnerable when authorities are not committed to viewpoint-neutral enforcement of the same rights for every person. When that standard is eroded, you are safe only so long as the authorities are on your side. And the more severely collective action is repressed, the more isolated everyone is. That makes everyone weaker and therefore genuinely more vulnerable.

NOTHING I HAVE SAID requires that you agree with protesters who consider the war in Gaza genocide, nor with pro-life protesters who consider abortion genocide, nor with any other protest. It only requires agreement that everyone should enjoy a right to protest—not just formal permission to protest, but permission that holds up when protesters do what protesters do. It cannot be that there is a right to protest just so long as protesters avoid saying or doing anything inflammatory, uncivil, or outrageous.

That, in turn, requires a culture of toleration, even for what seems at times intolerable. This is psychologically hard, even physically taxing. But we should demand this toleration, especially by those in authority who have the power to coercively interfere. If this vision seems too permissive, it is worth stressing an inherent limit: whatever right protesters claim for themselves is a right they are also claiming for their enemies. That is the way it is if one expects institutional protection of a right. Anything less is a conditional license, subject to the whims of the powerful.

This principle has to be defended on campus, against those who believe protests are incompatible with, or merely disruptive of, the social and educational mission of the university. And it has to be defended externally, against those who want to undermine academic freedom and freedom of speech broadly. Over the last year, universities did not come close to exploring the outer boundaries of what they could permit. We must demand they do, since nothing short of our commitment to democracy, the mission of the university, and the commons itself is at stake. **BR**

The November 1969 Mobilization to End the War rally in Washington, D.C. Image: Getty Images

HOW WE WON

Lessons from a Vietnam peace activist

David Cortright

WHEN NEWS OF THE END of the Vietnam War arrived, immortalized in images of U.S. helicopters lifting off from the roofs of Saigon, many who had worked for years to end the carnage gathered spontaneously in public places. I had joined the movement in 1968 as an active-duty soldier, and spent my time in the army organizing protests and circulating petitions and underground newspapers among fellow GIs. In Washington, D.C., that day, hundreds of us — veterans, draft resisters, students, community activists — streamed into Lafayette Square in front of the White House, the park where the first protest against the war had occurred a decade earlier.

There was no program or speech making. People just wandered about, in small groups or alone, speaking softly, averting eyes, holding back tears, in a collective mood of grief over the millions who had died but also relief that the slaughter, at last, was over. We hoped that our collective struggles had made a difference in ending a war that never should have been fought.

Five decades later, the consensus is firm: we had. Over the years, scholars have documented the many influences of peace protest in altering U.S. policy. As Carolyn Eisenberg affirms in her recent history, *Fire and Rain,* "Waves of mass demonstrations, accompanied by growing resistance inside the military, ongoing electoral activity, and lobbying efforts on Capitol Hill imposed significant constraints on presidential decision making." Over the course of the war, as the pressure intensified, White House decisions were increasingly based on concerns about public opinion and antiwar action.

Today, amid the political devastation in Washington, examining how peace protesters confronted the U.S. war machine holds vital lessons. What can we learn from the movement of fifty years ago for the present challenge—building a national movement to counter Trump and save American democracy?

"**THE SINGLE MOST IMPORTANT INFLUENCE** on a civil resistance campaign's success," argues political scientist Erica Chenoweth, "is the scale and range of popular participation." This includes not only organizing large national demonstrations but building grassroots networks in local communities. By that standard, the struggle against the war in Indochina—the largest, most sustained and intensive antiwar campaign in American history—was a success.

1967 was the year that the movement started to demonstrate the full extent of its power. In April Martin Luther King Jr. issued his famous "Declaration of Independence from the War in Vietnam" before thousands of listeners at New York's Riverside Church. Ten days later he led hundreds of thousands of peace protesters on a march to the United Nations headquarters in New York. King was excoriated for breaking with President Lyndon Johnson on Vietnam and thereby costing the civil rights movement White House support, but his firm moral indictment of the war had a powerful impact in deepening antiwar opposition, especially within religious communities. Six months later, in October, was the March on the Pentagon, one of the earliest large-scale demonstrations in Washington.

After seeing the massive press attention the March had garnered, the White House launched a media blitz of its own, claiming military success in the war. Commanding General William Westmoreland and U.S. Ambassador to Saigon Ellsworth Bunker were summoned to Washington to declare, on NBC's *Meet the Press*, that victory was within sight. Events on the battlefield would soon prove them wrong. Within two months of Westmoreland and Bunker's interview came the cataclysmic Tet Offensive, in which Vietnamese liberation forces launched a series of coordinated attacks across South Vietnam. Televised scenes of the bloodbath burst the bubble of raised expectations, and public confidence in Johnson's conduct of the war plummeted.

Liberal opponents of the war were already setting plans in motion. Americans for Democratic Action, a group previously supportive of

Johnson's Vietnam policy, launched an audacious electoral campaign to unseat the warmaking president, working with thousands of student volunteers to support the antiwar senator Eugene McCarthy as a candidate in the Democratic Party primary in New Hampshire, the first contest to be held. The little-known challenger polled a remarkable 42 percent of the vote—an "astonishing psychological victory," writes historian Charles DeBenedetti, that stunned Johnson and the Washington political establishment.

A combination of tactics—bodies in the streets and votes in ballot boxes—forced Washington's hand.

In March, still reeling from McCarthy's primary performance, Johnson made two shocking announcements: one, he would not run for re-election, and two, he was ordering a partial bombing halt in Vietnam and the start of peace negotiations. Weeks later, the White House also rejected a request made by Westmoreland for 206,000 additional troops, fearful that continued escalation would cause further civil unrest and an increase in already widespread draft resistance. Though it would take several agonizing years—and two more presidents—for the United States to fully withdraw and negotiate an agreement, these events marked the beginning of the end.

No one expected then that antiwar protest and electoral action would have such dramatic results. What we know now is that each tactic could not have succeeded without the other—that it was the combination of bodies in the streets and votes in ballot boxes that delivered the one-two punch that forced Washington's hand.

The nascent anti-Trump resistance appears to be taking the first steps toward this strategy. The enormous Hands Off protests of April 5, which saw millions of people march and rally at more than 1,300 individual events, were a dramatic display of the power of mass mobilization. Four days prior, anti-Trump organizers scored an important electoral success when the progressive Judge Susan Crawford won a Wisconsin Supreme Court election in which the White House, hoping to control the state's future electoral outcomes, actively backed her Republican opponent (and Elon Musk attempted to literally buy the election). As activists at the national level and in local districts explore similar targeted challenges in the months and years ahead, they will need to continue to harness the energy in the streets.

PRESIDENT RICHARD NIXON came into office with a promise to end the war, but once taking power he instead chose to continue the fighting—and in many ways, ratcheted it up. Nixon planned to threaten massive military escalation if Hanoi did not accept U.S. terms in the negotiations, a concept he described to his senior aide H. R. Haldeman as the "madman theory" of diplomacy. To impress the Vietnamese and their Soviet supporters of his seriousness, Nixon increased the operational readiness of U.S. nuclear forces and placed nuclear-armed B-52 bombers on alert status.

The peace movement responded to Nixon with a massive wave of protest, culminating in the historic Vietnam Moratorium of October 1969, which called for people to pause business as usual and engage in local action for peace—a concept both innovative and extremely popular. As soon as it was created, the idea caught on like wildfire, winning the endorsement of trade unions and professional associations, prominent intellectuals and artists, and former officials and members of Congress. On the day of the Moratorium, an estimated two million Americans participated in local activities, ranging from a gathering of 100,000 people on the Boston Common to rallies and prayer vigils in hundreds of cities and towns. A month later, the organizers of the Moratorium joined with the New Mobilization Committee to End the War in Vietnam to bring hundreds of thousands of marchers to the capital.

Nixon was shaken. Previously, he had declared that "under no circumstances will I be affected whatever" by protest. But now, just months into his presidency, the antiwar movement had applied so much pressure he was forced to change policy. As he later admitted in his memoir, "Although publicly I continued to ignore the raging antiwar controversy, I had to face the fact that it had probably destroyed the credibility of my ultimatum to Hanoi."

Like Nixon, Trump is not immune to mounting political opposition from the "radical left lunatics" he claims to ignore. In the first months of his presidency, after facing protests and court challenges, the White House backed off on some of its initial measures, halting its freeze on federal grant and loan programs and cuts to the federal health program for 9/11 survivors. If confronted with persistent mass protest and political pressure, the administration will be forced to abandon still more of its agenda.

———————————

WHEN NIXON SENT TROOPS to Cambodia in April 1970, campuses and communities exploded with protest. At Kent State University, Ohio National Guard troops fired into a crowd of unarmed demonstrators and killed four students, sparking an even larger convulsion of protest. Five days after the killings, more than a hundred thousand people gathered in D.C., and the national student strike soon spread to at least 883 campuses.

The furious upheaval in response to Cambodia and Kent State prompted Congress to act. In late 1970, the Senate approved the Cooper-Church Amendment, which cut off funds for further ground operations in Cambodia. The stirring of Congressional opposition was a significant factor in persuading the administration to accelerate the withdrawal of troops.

Washington, inundated with protests, had become a "besieged city," wrote Henry Kissinger. He and other unhappy and panicked executive officials moved into the basement bomb shelter of the White House. Nixon, for his part, faced "unbearable pressures," wrote Haldeman, "which caused him to order wiretaps and activate the plumbers [a secret break-in and dirty tricks squad] in response to antiwar moves" — events that marked the "beginning of his downward slide toward Watergate." In the moment, few activists could have imagined their resistance was having such dramatic effects. But time showed that their actions had set the stage for Nixon's eventual political downfall.

———————————

AS MASS DEMONSTRATIONS CONTINUED in 1971, an authoritative and influential voice joined the movement in force: the soldiers who had served. In April of that year, members of Vietnam Veterans Against the War (VVAW) descended on Washington, D.C., for several days of action, culminating in a gripping ceremony in which hundreds of fatigue-uniformed combat veterans, many in wheelchairs or on crutches, tossed their war medals and ribbons onto the steps of the Capitol Building.

Their dramatic performance received front-page national newspaper coverage and was a lead story on network news broadcasts, further turning public opinion against the war. Haldeman complained that media coverage of the veterans was "killing us," and that the White House was "getting pretty well chopped up" by the press. The protests drove Nixon crazy, driving him further toward the lawless actions that led to Watergate.

Like Nixon, Trump is not immune to the mounting political opposition he claims to ignore.

VVAW's efforts, which lasted until the war's end, turned out to be crucial. But organizing the veterans into an effective political force did not come about overnight. For years, civilian antiwar activists had worked patiently with already-politicized veterans to create coffeehouses outside major domestic military bases, which became centers for antiwar action and culture. Civilian legal aid groups provided support for veterans who were falsely accused of planning violent acts and GI resisters like myself who were punished for speaking out against the war. None of this could have come about without the realization that widespread veterans' support was going to be necessary to end the war.

Given the current administration's disdain for people in the military and the deep cuts imposed on the Department of Veteran Affairs and other federal agencies, opportunities may exist for engaging the military community today. If the administration attempts to use the military for illegal purposes, we may find that veterans, once again, will need to stand beside us.

As the last U.S. troops were leaving Vietnam, the Nixon administration tried to stave off defeat by providing more weapons and money to its beleaguered client regimes in Saigon and Phnom Penh. Peace activists responded with a major lobbying campaign, and mobilized pressure in the home districts of Congress members with a steady stream of telegrams, letters, and protests outside congressional offices. Bolstered by a growing number of members elected on an antiwar platform, Congress listened. In 1973, it approved landmark legislation terminating all U.S. military activity "in or over or from off the shores" of Indochina, marking the definitive end of all U.S. military operations in Southeast Asia.

The movement's next step was to challenge White House requests for billions of dollars of additional military aid for the two faltering regimes. The lobbying campaign culminated in 1975 when President Gerald Ford requested urgent military assistance for the states to continue fighting. Graham Martin, the U.S. ambassador in Saigon, cabled Congress to urge support for the funding request, but after thousands of activists gathered in Washington for an antiwar assembly to block the aid, Congress rejected it, sealing the fate of the South Vietnamese and Cambodian governments.

The rejection of military funding, Martin later admitted in a testimony to Congress, was due to a "beautifully orchestrated" lobbying effort by the Indochina Resource Center and related peace groups. "Those individuals deserve enormous credit for a very effective performance," he said. It was "the constancy of the drumming in day after day" and "the building of the pressure from the constituencies" that ended U.S. involvement in the war.

THE VIETNAM PEACE MOVEMENT kept up its drumbeat for a decade before it won its final demand. Can the anti-Trump resistance muster the same kind of energy?

To be sure, 2025 is not 1967. Back then, the draft put the war front and center in all of our lives, affecting millions of young men forced to serve—and their families and friends—throughout the country. And even as the draft was ending, the protests continued, driven by a unifying motivation: to save lives, both American and Vietnamese, and stop the seemingly endless slaughter our government was unleashing. Today, the breadth of the Trump administration's depredations, and the dizzying speed at which they have come, have flung many issues onto the table all at once: cuts to essential services, the shuttering of entire government agencies, unlawful deportations of migrants and Palestinian rights activists, open defiance of the Constitution and federal courts—the list goes on.

The resistance movement that has emerged is broad, but it is also multisectoral and individualized, addressing many specific issues among many particular groups and constituencies. Black leaders spoke at the April 5 events, but the crowds were mostly white. Labor leaders took the podium, but connecting unions' focus on workplace issues with emerging threats to their very existence remains a work in progress.

Still, there are signs that a unified opposition could bloom from out of this ground. It's worth remembering that April's Hands Off rallies took place just months after Trump resumed office. The fact that a national protest featuring such an array of groups—many of which are far from natural allies—could be organized at all is a sign that there is already real, widespread resistance. If sustained and enlarged, it could alter the current political landscape as profoundly as did its predecessors in 1967. But this will require channeling the energy the masses have unleashed into organized political action.

How to do so? First, by taking another cue from the Vietnam protesters: figuring out where best to apply the pressure. With Washington controlled by a Republican regime actively dismantling the government in front of a mostly feckless Democratic opposition, the near-term prospects for conventional lobbying at the national level are limited. The focus should instead be to build the capacity for political mobilization at the local level. Activists will be more effective if they concentrate on building grassroots networks and campaigns in local districts, which will lay the foundation for electoral and legislative action in the months and years ahead. Their primary challenge will be harmonizing the many voices of protest into a mighty chorus of defiance. The movement has a common slogan—"Hands Off!"—but to date, no unifying agenda and strategic vision to accompany it.

As the scale of the crisis deepens, those stakes might snap into focus. Already, the White House and Republican leaders in Congress are moving to implement massive budget cuts targeting essential health care programs like Medicaid and Obamacare. Reduced funding for these programs would greatly impact tens of millions of people. Brought together, they would represent the largest, most diverse, political opposition in the country. If organizations focus on preserving Medicaid, VA benefits, and other health programs, they could create a true big-tent coalition—one large enough to hold the likes of working-class people, seniors, veterans, and perhaps even moderate Republicans.

The Vietnam movement had a simple set of demands: Stop the Bombing. Out Now. It succeeded because it paired the relentless drumming of antiwar protest with the savvy use of institutional politics. Today we need to employ similar tactics: constant protest nationally and locally, political engagement to influence electoral and legislative outcomes, and, to tie the two together, unifying demands that attract broad popular support. Already, a couple have emerged: Stop the Cuts. Hands Off. What remains is to bring together a coalition strong enough to take on the White House. **BR**

CONTRIBUTORS

Gianpaolo Baiocchi is Professor of Sociology at New York University, where he directs the Urban Democracy Lab. His most recent book is *We, the Sovereign*.

Benjamin Balthaser is Associate Professor of Multi-Ethnic U.S. Literature at Indiana University, South Bend. His latest book is *Citizens of the Whole World: Anti-Zionism and the Cultures of the American Jewish Left*.

Emily Baughan is senior lecturer at the University of Sheffield and author of *Saving the Children: Humanitarianism, Internationalism, and Empire*.

Eric Blanc is an organizer and Assistant Professor of Labor Studies at Rutgers. His latest book is *We Are the Union: How Worker-to-Worker Organizing Is Revitalizing Labor and Winning Big*.

David Cortright is a Vietnam-era veteran, peace activist, and professor emeritus at the Keough School of Global Affairs at the University of Notre Dame. His many books include *Soldiers in Revolt: GI Resistance During the Vietnam War*.

Marcus Gadson is incoming Associate Professor of Law at the University of North Carolina at Chapel Hill and author of *Sedition: How America's Constitutional Order Emerged from Violent Crisis*.

John Ganz is a columnist at *The Nation* and author of *When the Clock Broke: Con Men, Conspiracists, and How America Cracked Up in the Early 1990s*.

Lily Geismer is Professor of History at Claremont McKenna College and coeditor, with Brent Cebul, of *Mastery and Drift: Professional-Class Liberals since the 1960s*.

Alex Gourevitch is Associate Professor of Political Science at Brown and author of *From Slavery to the Cooperative Commonwealth: Labor and Republican Liberty in the Nineteenth Century*.

Kelly Hayes is a Menominee writer and organizer. She is coauthor, with Mariame Kaba, of *Let This Radicalize You: Organizing and the Reciprocal Revolution of Care*.

Aziz Huq is Frank and Bernice J. Greenberg Professor of Law at the University of Chicago and coauthor, with Tom Ginsburg, of *How to Save a Constitutional Democracy*.

Judith Levine is a journalist and commentator. Her latest book, co-authored with Erica R. Meiners, is *The Feminist and the Sex Offender: Confronting Sexual Harm, Ending State Violence.*

Lisa L. Miller is Professor of Political Science at Rutgers University. She is completing a book called *The Myth of Checks and Balances and the American Democratic Deficit.*

Samuel Moyn is Chancellor Kent Professor of Law and History at Yale University. His latest book is *Liberalism Against Itself: Cold War Intellectuals and the Making of Our Times.*

Troy Nahumko is a writer based in Spain and author of *Stories Left in Stone: Trails and Traces in Cáceres.* His work has also appeared in *Counterpunch, The Toronto Star*, and *El País.*

Debbie Nathan is a journalist based in New York specializing in immigration, the U.S.-Mexico border, and sexual politics. Her reporting has also appeared in *The Intercept* and *The Nation.*

Maya Schenwar directs the Truthout Center for Grassroots Journalism and serves as *Truthout*'s editor at large and board president. She is author of *Locked Down, Locked Out: Why Prison Doesn't Work and How We Can Do Better.*

G. M. Tamás (1948–2023) was a Romanian-born Hungarian philosopher and dissident. After fleeing the Ceaușescu regime, he was elected to Hungary's Parliament in 1989. He later served as head of the Institute of Philosophy at the Hungarian Academy of Sciences and taught at several universities in the United States and Europe.